THE THEORY OF DEMOCRATIC ELITISM

A Critique

Peter Bachrach

UNIVERSITY
PRESS OF
AMERICA

© **1980 by Peter Bachrach**

University Press of America, Inc.™

P.O. Box 19101, Washington, DC 20036

ISBN: 0-8191-1185-6 Perfect
ISBN: 0-8191-1184-8 Case
Library of Congress Number: 80-5747

Foreword

LIKE SO MANY areas of human knowledge to-
day, the study of politics and political institutions is undergoing
significant changes. A quarter-century ago only a few voices
challenged the prevailing consensus regarding the methods of
political science, the choice of problems, and the relative weight
assigned to the "factors" shaping political events, actions, and behavior. Since then a revolution of uncertain proportions has occurred, one that has been variously described as "the behavioral
movement" or "social science." It has visibly altered the climate of
political science and it has deeply affected the outlook of the
political scientist. No longer does he believe that political science
is a self-contained field. It has become second nature for him to
utilize methods, concepts, and data drawn from a wide range of
academic disciplines, such as sociology, psychology, and economics.

A marked self-consciousness about methods of inquiry charac-
terizes much of the contemporary literature, whereas thirty years
ago only a few political scientists were troubled by this concern.
Today's political scientist is receptive to quantitative techniques,

eager to emphasize measurement, prepared to devise complex classifications of empirical data, ready to experiment with abstract models, and engrossed with the intricacies of preparing questionnaires and organizing surveys of public opinion. These changes in method have also affected the outlook and the language of political science. Where his predecessors talked of "comparative government," he is apt to talk of "comparative political systems"; where they referred to "the process of government," he prefers to examine "the theory of decision-making"; and where they spoke simply of "political theory," he will, more often than not, insist on a distinction between "normative theory" and "empirical theory" and, depending on his candor or concerns, will assert that his main interest lies with the latter. It is perhaps inevitable that a moderate reaction should set in and that questions should be raised among political scientists about whether they have not gone too far and too fast. There is an uneasiness that some settled issues ought to be reopened; that important features of politics have been ignored; that questions of choice and value have to be restored to a central position; and that the wonder of politics has been lost amidst the preoccupation with abstractions, graphs, and mathematical tables.

In the light of these changes and uncertainties there is good reason for political scientists and political theorists to reflect on the changing nature of their field of study and to report to a less specialized, but no less interested, audience how political events, practices, and behavior appear to the contemporary political scientist; what way or ways of looking at these matters he has found most useful and fruitful; and what problems he considers to be genuine and important.

This series of books was designed for such a purpose. The authors do not attempt to provide simply a digest of relevant facts, but to offer reflections and systematic analyses of the more significant and interesting areas of political science and political theory. Some concentrate upon familiar topics, such as federalism and political parties, but they seek to suggest the theoretically interesting problems raised by these traditional themes. Other studies, such as those dealing with political theory and ideology, proceed on a more theoretical plane, but with the explicit intention of indicating their relevance to the empirical concerns of political science. The standard set for this volume by Professor Bachrach and for all the others is, I hope, within the best tradition of political science: the standard of reflective inquiry and informed analysis.

Professor Bachrach deals with a theme as old as the Western tradition of politics itself: the controversy between elitism and democracy. Political philosophy was founded on this controversy; the shape of Plato's *Republic* was an outgrowth of his criticism of Athenian democracy. Although the dispute between democracy and elitism is an ancient one, it is important to recognize that over the centuries the arguments for both sides have varied and that the protagonists have given different contents to the key terms in the debate. Plato's case for a philosophical elite involved more than an attack upon democracy. It rejected simultaneously the claims of two other elitist positions, an aristocracy of birth and an oligarchy of wealth. Through a rigorous process of selection and education, Plato hoped to produce a new breed, a new kind of philosopher and a new kind of ruler. In the light of later theories of elitism, especially those inspired by Calvinism or by secular variants of it, it is worth noting that Plato never contended that his elite derived its legitimacy from some form of providential or historical inevitability.

Whereas classical political philosophy was launched with an attack upon democracy, modern political philosophy and its off-shoot, democratic theory, began with an assault upon a special form of elitism, the elitism of hereditary status and privilege. Neither Machiavelli nor Hobbes, two of the major founders of modern political theory, was a democrat, yet each was a powerful critic of hereditary aristocracy and, in the case of Hobbes, an advocate of equality. Rutherford's comment, "for no man cometh out of the womb with a diadem on his head, or a sceptre in his hand," pretty well summarized the early modern democrat's case against elitism. However, the case was far from being closed. The industrial, technological, and scientific revolutions of the nineteenth and twentieth centuries consigned the old aristocracies to the museum and transformed the bases of social and economic power. Saint-Simon was the first to proclaim a new elitism in the name of the organizational needs of science and industry and to argue that the democratic revolutions of the eighteenth century were obsolete before they had been consummated. The new world that was rapidly coming into being demanded the skills of the engineer, scientist, and administrator. A new elite, defined in terms of the functional needs of industrial society, was required. It followed that democracy, with its emphasis upon equality, popular participation, and the responsibility of the governors to the governed, was not only anachronistic but also dangerous. Decisions and policies were matters for expert determination rather than parliamentary divisions or electoral counts.

The defenders of liberal democracy tried to evade the logic of industrialism by clinging to the dogma that economic matters belonged to the province of "society" and, accordingly, were protected from political control by immunities erected to safeguard "private" life. The growth of large-scale industrial organization fostered by the corporate revolution of the last half of the nineteenth century quickly showed the inadequacies of the liberal democratic formulation; but the *coup de grace* came in the early twentieth century when it was discovered that the organizational revolution had quietly penetrated the structure of democracy and transformed it. Writers, such as Michels and Weber, thrust aside the rhetoric of democracy to expose a bureaucratized system manned primarily by elites. The situation was not ascribed to a conspiracy, but was viewed as the inevitable response to "mass democracy." Only organization could cope with the shapeless mass created by urbanization and industrialism. Inasmuch as organization was invariably equated with a hierarchical structure, the line of reasoning, which began by positing the existence of the masses and then deducing from it the necessity for organization, was bound to terminate in elitism.

The response of democratic theorists was surprisingly weak, possibly because the discovery of "the iron law of oligarchy" and its variants was announced in the name of social science. The tendency of most democratic theorists was to acknowledge that democratic politics, in varying degrees, was dominated by elites; they sought to escape the consequences of this admission by arguing that the sufficient condition of democracy was fulfilled if (a) the electorate were able to choose between competing elites, (b) the elites did not succeed in rendering their power hereditary or in preventing new social groups from gaining access to elite positions, (c) the elites had to draw support from shifting coalitions which would mean that no single form of power would become dominant, and (d) the elites dominating various areas of society, such as business, education, and the arts, did not form a common alliance.

This sketch constitutes the background to Professor Bachrach's analysis. In the course of his discussion, it becomes evident, I think, that democracy's troubles are only in part due to the presence of elites. The findings of empirical political and social science have seriously weakened the democratic faith in the qualities and capacities of citizens. The voter is presented in a highly unflattering light: poorly informed, prejudiced, and apathetic. Small wonder that some contemporary social scientists are beginning to sound like neo-Federalists as they warn against the latent "authoritarianism" of what used to be called "the lower orders" and suggest that the "stability" of the "political system" would be furthered if certain segments of the population did not vote or actively engage in political life. As the present study points out, some contemporary political and social scientists have exactly reversed the traditional democratic argument concerning what maintains and what threatens a democratic system. The former contend that the perpetuation of democracy depends on the ability of the elite to protect the system against the masses, while the traditional democratic argument identifies elites as one of the main dangers to the system.

In considering these problems, Professor Bachrach insists that the present position of elites in the United States can be offset only by the revitalization of political participation. Towards this end, he proposes a redefinition of the "political," one that is sufficiently comprehensive to include the concentrations of private power, such as the giant corporation, whose decisions affect society as profoundly as the decisions of government itself. The next step is to extend the idea and practices of democratic participation to these units. Although the present study does not profess to have solved all of the difficulties of democracy, it succeeds in formulating a set of significant issues and in compelling the reader to face the choice: either a revitalization of democratic participation or the acceptance of a state of affairs in which political decision-making is carried on with progressively less democratic control.

Sheldon S. Wolin

UNIVERSITY OF CALIFORNIA, BERKELEY

Preface

UNTIL QUITE RECENTLY democratic and elite theories were regarded as distinct and conflicting. While in their pure form they are still regarded as contradictory, there is, I believe, a strong if not dominant trend in contemporary political thought toward incorporating major elitist principles within democratic theory. As a result there is a new theory which I have called democratic elitism. This book is a historical and analytical examination of the theory, the chief purpose of which is to probe its soundness both as empirical and as normative theory.

I am indebted to Professor Louis Hartz of Harvard University for his encouragement during the initial stages of this study; and to Professor Morton Baratz of Bryn Mawr College, Professor Alfred Diamant of Haverford College, and to Professor Sheldon Wolin of the University of California for reading the manuscript and offering invaluable suggestions and criticisms. I am also indebted to Dean Alice Emerson and Mr. Charles Cooper of the University of Pennsylvania, Professor Eugene Schneider of Bryn Mawr College, and Mr. Richard Jenney of Haverford, Pennsylvania, for reading and criticizing various chapters.

I wish to thank the Rockefeller Foundation for its generous grant, without which the essay could not have been written. I also wish to express my appreciation to the editor of the *Journal of Politics* for permission to reprint the substance of Chapter Four which originally appeared in its pages.

P. B.

Table
of contents

xiii

4

ELITE CONSENSUS, 47

5

THE CONCEPT OF POLITICAL ELITE, 65

6

EQUALITY, 83

7

AN ALTERNATIVE APPROACH, 93

To H. B.

THE THEORY OF
Democratic Elitism
A Critique

I

Introduction

THIS BOOK is predicated upon the assumption that there is, in the normative sense, a fundamental distinction between democratic and elite theories. Therefore it is important at the outset to be clear as to the nature of the basic difference between these terms. It does not turn on the common supposition that elitism is "government by the few" and democracy "government by the people." The exigencies of life in the industrial and nuclear age necessitate that key and crucial political decisions in a democracy, as in totalitarian societies, be made by a handful of men. Those who lived through the agonizing days of the Cuban crisis, of the United States's confrontation of Soviet power, would be hard pressed to reach a contrary conclusion.[1] The issue for the democrat is not one of choosing between effective government and democratic government. If it were, democracy would be an untenable alternative.

[1] The force of C. Wright Mills's *Power Elite* (New York, 1956) is considerably diminished since the key decisions that he lists as being made by the elite are those, such as the bomb, Korea, Dien Bien Phu, which the President made and for which he was constitutionally responsible. See Daniel Bell, *End of Ideology* (Glencoe, Ill., 1960), p. 49.

1

Neither can democracy and elitism on a theoretical level be distinguished by characterizing the first as "government for the people" and the latter as "rule for the selfish interests of the rulers." Pláto's guardians, Veblen's technocrats, and Mannheim's intellectuals — to name a few elite types — were all conceived as possessing the ability to transcend selfish interest in ruling for the well-being of the community.[2] Indeed, the modern defense of elitism, as we shall see, is based primarily on the contention that the best interest of a free people, of civilization itself, depends upon the ability of the gifted to command the deference of the many for the well-being of all.

While elitism and democracy are similar in that the primary purpose of government for each is to safeguard and further the interest of the community, they differ fundamentally as to what this interest entails, and as to the role of government in securing it. All elite theories are founded on two basic assumptions: first, that the masses are inherently incompetent, and second, that they are, at best, pliable, inert stuff or, at worst, aroused, unruly creatures possessing an insatiable proclivity to undermine both culture and liberty. The indispensability of a dominant, creative elite is, of course, a corollary assumption basic to the philosophy of elitism. Elite theorists of all persuasions — revolutionary, liberal, conservative, and reactionary — rely equally upon the validity of this assumption, disagreeing only as to the political objectives toward which the elite-manipulated masses should be directed. Thus Lenin, for example, in viewing the common man as a helpless child hypnotized by bourgeois ideology, staked all on the ability of a highly dedicated and disciplined elite to break the bourgeois spell and lead the masses to the promised land. On the reactionary side, Ortega despaired for the fate of Western civilization unless the cultured elite managed to subdue the masses to a passive and deferential level suitable to the mediocrity of their nature.

The insistence upon the inequality of individual endowment is not the point upon which democratic theory challenges elitism.

[2] Being "realists," both Mosca and Pareto were exceptions in this regard, holding that governing elites ruled primarily in their own interest. See Chapter 2.

Indeed, the democrat, as Jefferson's letters to Adams attest,[3] looks upon men who excel in all endeavors — the elites — as essential to a vital and free society. But unlike the elitist, the democrat cannot justify imposing his view of a hierarchical ordering of human attributes by which society can make a definitive judgment upon the worth of a human being. His views, based upon his value preferences, are, of course, firm as to what constitutes the good life. But being unable to claim that his values are true for all men and for all time, he is unwilling to impose them upon his fellow men. Paradoxically, the skepticism of the democrat toward his ability to make this claim supports and is supported by his moral and absolute belief in the equality of man. (In Holmesian terms, this belief is one of his "can't helps.") The idea of common humanity implicit in the concept of the equality of man [4] is also incompatible with the insistence in elite theory upon categorization of man into higher and lower orders. Thus, the democratic ideal encourages the greatest utilization of the capabilities of individuals in the interest of the community, but in sharp contrast to elite theory, each individual's judgment on the general direction and character of political policies is given weight equal with all others.

For democratic theory, especially classical democratic theory, conceives the public interest in terms of both results and process. Thus public interest is measured by the soundness of the decisions reached in the light of the needs of the community *and* by the scope of public participation in reaching them. A prudent electorate would undoubtedly reject the good office of a benevolent despot — either in the guise of the philosopher king or in the robes of the lofty judge — on the grounds that his benevolence would soon become corrupted by power. But even on the assumption that his benevolence was beyond corruptibility, his services would be rejected. For, as J. S. Mill asks, "What sort of human beings can be formed under such a regime? What development can either their thinking or their active faculties attain under

[3] *The Life and Selected Writings of Thomas Jefferson* (Modern Library edition, New York, 1944), pp. 632–34.

[4] For a discussion of this subject, see Karl Mannheim, *Essays on Sociology of Culture* (London, 1956), pp. 176–78.

it?" [5] Not to engage in the political affairs of one's country would result, Mill answers, in the stunting of man's intellectual and moral capacities and in the narrowing and dwarfing of his sentiments.[6] In a passage which is uncomfortably relevant to present-day democracies, he states: "Leaving things to the Government, like leaving them to Providence, is synonymous with caring nothing about them, accepting their results, when disagreeable, as visitations of Nature. With the exception, therefore, of a few studious men who take an intellectual interest in speculation for its own sake, the intelligence and sentiments of a whole people are given up to the material interests, and, when these are provided for, to the amusement and ornamentation, of private life." [7]

Benevolent despotism thus becomes a contradiction in terms; and it has been argued that malevolent despotism would be preferable, at least up to the point where it engenders opposition, creating intellectual concern and moral indignation.[8]

The emphasis in classical democratic theory upon citizen participation in all aspects of public affairs is based on the premise that such involvement is an essential means to the full development of individual capacities. The self-developmental approach of the democrat has a common strain with the educational philosophies of such diverse men as Jesus, Freud, and Dewey. For each in his own way argued that man could know truth, and thus be freer than before, only through discovering it by himself. This did not preclude guidance and encouragement of elites in the educational process, but, contrary to the premise of elitism, it did preclude a relationship of elite domination and creativity, and of non-elite submissiveness and passivity.

It is often said, notwithstanding Aristotle's famous dictum that man is a political animal, that man's energies and interests are absorbed primarily in his personal life, and that, consequently,

---

[5] *Representative Government* (Everyman edition), p. 203.

[6] *Ibid.*, p. 204.

[7] *Ibid.*, p. 205.

[8] Along similar lines, de Tocqueville favorably contrasts the tyranny of European monarchs with the tyranny of omnipotent majority opinion. See *Democracy in America*, ed. Phillips Bradley (New York, 1945).

politics, except under unusual conditions, is bound to be of marginal interest to him. Thus, if self-development is the road to the good life, it must be achieved, especially for ordinary men, within the private sector. Classical democratic theory challenges this assumption that privatization of life is endemic to most men, holding, as Mill argued, that confinement of man within the concerns of his private needs and pleasures is artificially to circumscribe and impinge upon the development of his capabilities; that the full fruition of his faculties requires the responsibility and stimulus which come from grappling with problems that reach beyond his immediate personal interest. Mill's hope, and that of A. D. Lindsay and Ernest Barker after him, was that the democratization and liberalization of society would afford all men an opportunity to become involved through acceptance of public responsibility and thus to become alive to broader and more enriching facets of life than "material interests and . . . amusement and ornamentation of private life." [9] To what extent this hope is utopian for modern industrial societies is a question which will concern us in the course of this essay.

The fundamental difference between elitists and democrats, then, is reflected not only in their conflicting approaches to the question "Who should be responsible for determining basic policy questions of the body politic?" but also, and perhaps more significantly, in their diverse approaches as to what constitutes the public interest. Elitist theories view the latter problem in one-dimensional terms: the general interest is realized when governmental policy is in accord with the judgment of the elite. The emphasis, in short, is placed upon the attainment of enlightened public policy; the elite is enlightened, thus its policy is bound to be the public interest. Viewed two-dimensionally, classical democratic theory conceives of the public interest in terms of both ends and means. "To secure these rights," states the Declaration of Independence, "government is instituted among men," but

---

[9] For two recent and forceful statements of this position, see Graeme Duncan and Steven Lukes, "New Democracy," *Political Studies* (vol. II, June, 1963), pp. 156–77; and Edward Davis, "Cost of Realism: Contemporary Restatement of Democracy," *Western Political Quarterly* (vol. 18, March, 1964), pp. 37–46.

if the rights secured are not actually utilized by the people in the political process, it cannot be said that the public interest has been realized. Government by the people, strictly interpreted, is today impossible, but widespread public participation in the political process is perhaps still possible. In light of this ideal, government for the people is measured, to a large extent, by its effect on the health of the political process itself. Conceived circularly, democratic governmental policy enhances the interest of the people and, in turn, is reflected in a sustained, broadly based citizen interest and participation in politics. And the interaction of means and ends — of process and policy — stimulates and encourages the self-development of a free people.

Classical democratic theory is no doubt still pleasing to the democratic mind. But to what extent, if at all, is it meaningful for mass democratic societies such as ours? Nostalgia for the New England town meeting of colonial days and for the vital local government described by de Tocqueville in the Jacksonian period is understandable. But viable democratic theory can hardly be built upon a dream that has not the remotest chance of being realized. Certainly it is not sufficient to show, especially when accompanied by accusations of sacrilege, that the theory of democratic elitism has departed from the classical model.[10]

Of course democratic theory must provide an ideal upon which the political system can be judged and toward which a free people can strive. To be content with an explanatory model of democracy, or, indeed, of polyarchy — albeit useful — is to be left aimless, without direction and perspective, and without the inspiration and fire to reach that which is presently unattainable. "Certainly all historical experience confirms the truth," declared Max Weber, "that man would not have attained the possible unless time and again he had reached out for the impossible."[11] However, to lose sight of reality in political theorizing is to invite indifference and boredom. The theorist must take heed, in

[10] This criticism applies especially to the otherwise excellent articles by Duncan and Lukes, and Davis, *ibid*.

[11] H. H. Gerth and C. Wright Mills (eds.), *From Max Weber: Essays in Sociology* (Galaxy paperback, New York, 1958), p. 128.

short, that in "reaching out for the impossible" — in an effort to change society to what might be — he is firmly anchored in the stuff of what is. Put within the context of the problem of this essay, he must fully recognize the elite-mass nature of modern industrial society and the implications of this fact for democratic theory.

In spite of the wide divergence in approach and methodological techniques in the investigation of the decision-making process in communal and organizational life in the United States,[12] scholars — political scientists and sociologists alike — conclude that "the key political, economic, and social decisions" are made by "tiny minorities." [13] In large part, this phenomenon is attributable to the politically unorganized, fragmented, and passive state of the great majority of the people.[14] "Mass democracy has, through its very nature," observed E. H. Carr, "thrown up on all sides specialized groups of leaders — what are sometimes called elites. Everywhere, in government, in political parties, in trade unions, in co-operatives, these indispensable elites have taken shape with startling rapidity." [15] And, according to Robert Dahl, "It is difficult — nay impossible — to see how it could be otherwise in large political systems." [16]

Owing to the dramatic growth of elite power, most leading theorists regard the self-developmental approach to democracy as

[12] See Peter Bachrach and Morton S. Baratz, "Two Faces of Power," *American Political Science Review* (vol. 56, December, 1962), pp. 947-48.

[13] Robert Dahl, "Power, Pluralism and Democracy: A Modest Proposal," a paper delivered at the 1964 annual meeting of the American Political Science Association, Chicago, p. 3.

[14] E. E. Schattschneider, *The Semisovereign People* (New York, 1960), pp. 20-42; and Fred I. Greenstein, *The American Party System and the American People* (Englewood Cliffs, N.J., 1963), pp. 10-14.

[15] *New Society* (Boston, 1951), p. 72.

[16] Robert Dahl, "Power, Pluralism and Democracy: A Modest Proposal," *op. cit.*, p. 3. Also see Giovanni Sartori, *Democratic Theory* (Detroit, 1962), pp. 112, 123. Emphasizing the impact of specialization in the industrial age upon the rapid growth of elites, Suzanne Keller writes, "The democratic ethos notwithstanding, men must become accustomed to bigger, more extensive, and more specialized elites in their midst as long as industrial societies keep growing and becoming more specialized. . . ." *Beyond the Ruling Class* (New York, 1963), pp. 71-72.

an anachronism.[17] To continue to advocate such a theory in to-day's world, it is argued, is bound to foster cynicism toward democracy as it becomes evident that the gap between the reality and the ideal cannot be closed.[18] Thus it is said that there is no alternative but to recast democracy, emphasizing the stable, con-stitutional, and liberal nature of the system of elite pluralism; the competitiveness of political elites, their accountability to the electorate at periodic elections; and the open, multiple points of access to elite power for those who bother to organize to voice their grievances and demands. In this view elites become the core of democratic or, if one prefers, polyarchical theory. To be sure, the ordinary man still plays a role in the system since he has the freedom to vote, to bring pressure upon political elites, and to attempt himself to rise to an elite position. But by and large he does, and is expected to, remain relatively passive — in fact the health of the system depends upon it. For if he becomes too ac-tive, too aroused in politics, awakening the alienated, the apathetic masses of the cities and the rednecks of rural communities, po-litical equilibrium is thrown out of balance and the demagogue finds greater opportunity to challenge successfully the power of established elites. Widespread mass support of totalitarian move-ments in prewar Europe and the rise of powerful proletarian-based Communist parties in postwar France and Italy, of Peronism in Argentina and McCarthyism in the United States have badly shaken the confidence of liberals in the cause of de-mocracy. The increased power of established elites in democratic countries consequently has not been entirely disapproved of from this quarter. In fact, reminiscent of the views of de Tocqueville, Burke, and de Maistre, elites are once again regarded not only as the energetic and creative forces of society, but, above all, as the source which sustains the system. The relationship of elites to masses is, in a vital way, reversed from classical theory: masses,

---

[17] Roland Pennock is an exception. See his "Democracy and Leadership," in *Democracy Today*, ed. William N. Chambers and Robert H. Salisbury (New York, 1962), pp. 122–59 [formerly published as *Democracy in the Mid-Twentieth Century* (St. Louis, 1960), pp. 122–59].

[18] See, for example, Dahl, *op. cit.*, p. 14. This problem is discussed in Chapter 6.

not elites, become the potential threat to the system, and elites, not masses, become its defender.

An analysis of this theory, which I have called democratic elitism, is the primary purpose of this essay. On the existential level, the meaning of such concepts as "political elite," "political accountability," "equality," and "interest" must be explored. I am interested not only in clarifying the meaning of these terms within the framework of democratic-elite theory, but also, and more importantly, in appraising the extent to which these concepts and the theory as a whole are realistic. If democratic theory had to be revised to be more in line with a rapidly changing society, has the revision successfully integrated the democratic and elitist parts of the theory? On the normative plane, what principles does the theory embrace and defend? If the self-developmental ideal has been necessarily scuttled in the name of reality, what values have taken its place and whom do they benefit? Critically put, is it possible to fashion a democratic theory for a political system in which "we have to reckon with minorities who count for much and lead, and with majorities who do not count for much and follow"? [19]

In the following chapters I have attempted to answer these questions, concluding generally that democratic elitism, as an empirical theory, is basically unsound; and that viewed normatively, it fails to meet the essential political needs of twentieth-century man. In the last chapter I have suggested an alternative interpretation of democracy which departs from both democratic elitism and classical theory.

[19] Sartori, *op. cit.*, p. 98.

2

The precursors:
Mosca and Schumpeter

STRIPPED of its anti-democratic verbiage, the later chapters of Mosca's *Ruling Class* [1] can be said to constitute the first formulation of democratic elitism.[2] The most crucial problem confronting civilization, in the eyes of both Mosca and Pareto, was how to avert the catastrophe of a "demagogic plutocracy," especially under the guise of socialism. In line with the de Tocquevillian tradition of the time, they sharply distinguished liberalism from democracy, embracing the former and regarding the latter as an effective vehicle, albeit a myth, for demagogic takeover. Thus identified as a dangerous means and

[1] *The Ruling Class: Elementi Di Scienza Politica*, ed. Arthur Livingston (New York, 1939).

[2] James Meisel, the author of the excellent work on Mosca, believes that Mosca has not really "arrived" in the United States. For, he states, "the democrats, much as his theory of balance and juridical defense may please them, will continue to loathe Mosca because of his doctrine of ruling class with its aristocratic overtones." *The Myth of the Ruling Class* (Ann Arbor, 1958), p. 364. In Suzanne Keller's view, Mosca and Pareto are historically interesting, but not pertinent for the present. *Beyond the Ruling Class* (New York, 1963), p. 13.

catalyst to socialist [3] revolution, democracy came under heavy fire from the elitists. It was ridiculed, on the one hand, as myth: "We need not linger," declared Pareto, "on the fiction of 'popular representation' — poppycock grinds no flour"; [4] and on the other, as capable of producing "the worst type of political organization and anonymous tyranny of those who win in the elections and speak in the name of the people." [5] To regard democracy as both myth and tyranny appears on its face inconsistent, but as Sorel vividly argued and Lenin skillfully demonstrated, the power of myth in the hands of a dedicated and shrewd elite can indeed be lethal.

Unlike Pareto, whose scathing remarks on majority rule, equality, and the like continued unsubsided throughout his lifetime and who had little difficulty in joining the fascist camp, Mosca eventually saw that "representative government" was an essential ingredient in solving the problem of political stability; that although in its unadulterated form, democracy leads to instability and tyranny,[6] under elite rule it becomes an anti-revolutionary force, assuring political stability and the maintenance of liberty.

I

The first edition of Mosca's *Elementi* in 1896, in contrast with the enlarged edition twenty-seven years later, is clearly an elitist and anti-democratic tract. In common with all elite theorists, Mosca in striking fashion asserts at the outset that "in all societies . . . two classes of people appear — a class that rules and a class that is ruled." [7] To say that all societies are divided into those who govern and those who are governed is hardly shocking, but he adds an anti-democratic bite to it by insisting that "the first class, always the less numerous, performs all political functions, monopolizes power and enjoys the advantages that power

[3] See Meisel, *ibid.,* pp. 286–87.

[4] Vilfredo Pareto, *The Mind and Society,* trans. Arthur Livingston (New York, 1935), #2244. Also see Mosca, p. 477.

[5] *The Ruling Class,* p. 157.

[6] *Ibid.,* pp. 150–52.

[7] *Ibid.,* p. 50.

brings, whereas the second, the more numerous class, is directed and controlled by the first, in a manner that is now more or less legal, now more or less arbitrary and violent. . . ." [8] Thus society is governed — irrespective of its political form, as Mosca continually reminds us — for the interest of the minority by means of manipulation and violence.[9]

Neither Mosca nor Pareto holds that the masses have no influence on the ruling class, or, in Pareto's terms, "the governing elite." Mosca pointed out that a certain amount of political pressure is exerted "from the passions by which they [the masses] are swayed," [10] and Pareto, in speaking of a parliamentary form of government, conceded that the governing elite "must now and again bend the knee to the whims of the ignorant and domineering sovereigns or parliaments, but they are soon back at their tenacious, patient, never-ending work, which is of much the greater consequence." [11] For Mosca the inevitability of minority domination was explained by its organization and unity of purpose. "An organized minority, obeying a single impulse," he stated, is irresistible against an unorganized majority, in which each individual "stands alone before the totality of the organized minority. A hundred men acting uniformly in concert, with a common understanding, will triumph over a thousand men who are not in accord and can therefore be dealt with one by one." [12]

---

[8] *Ibid.*

[9] "What happens," writes Mosca, "in other forms of government — namely, that an organized minority imposes its will on the disorganized majority — happens also and to perfection, whatever the appearance to the contrary, under the representative system. When we say that the voters 'choose' their representative, we are using a language that is very inexact. The truth is that the representative *has himself elected* by the voters . . ." (p. 154). Also see pp. 477–78.

In the same vein Pareto held: "The evolution toward 'democracy' seems to stand in strict correlation with the increased use of that instrument of governing which involves resort to artifice and to the machine; as against the instrument of force." In a democracy "the primary instrument of government is the manipulation of political followings. . . ." *Mind and Society*, #2259.

[10] *The Ruling Class*, p. 51.

[11] *Mind and Society*, #2253.

[12] *The Ruling Class*, p. 51.

In addition to the advantages of organization and cohesion, the ruling class, Mosca tells us, tends to monopolize the talented for their members, and unlike the masses possess qualities of "certain material, intellectual or even moral superiority, or else," he adds significantly, "they are the heirs of individuals who possessed such qualities." [13] Thus he approaches the Achilles heel of all ruling classes – their propensity to become hereditary, to solidify and die. In cutting off the "circulation of elites" from below, internal decay inevitably ensues, old capacities become unable to meet changing conditions; and simultaneously, the unity and vitality of insurgent forces from below begin to gather strength.

The assumption that it was imperative for the survival of any ruling class to keep abreast of and reflect the shifting forces – economic, social, intellectual, and religious – of society was basic to Mosca's thought. Unlike Marx, he did not attempt to explain their interrelationship or their origins but simply accepted their existence. However, in an extremely interesting passage on the rise and fall of ruling classes, Mosca approaches the grandeur of Marx's dialectic. He writes:

> The whole history of civilized mankind comes down to a conflict between the tendency of dominant elements to monopolize political power and transmit possession of it by inheritance, and the tendency toward a dislocation of old forces and an insurgence of new forces; and this conflict produces an unending ferment of endosmosis and exosmosis between the upper classes and certain portions of the lower. Ruling classes decline inevitably when they cease to find scope for the capacities through which they rose to power, when they can no longer render the social services which they once rendered, or when their talents and the services they render lose in importance in the social environment in which they live.[14]

Pareto's celebrated theory of the circulation of elites does not add much, other than the phrase itself, to Mosca's formulation of the principle. Social equilibrium, according to Pareto, is dependent upon a sufficient circulation of talented and ambitious individuals from non-elites to elites. But apparently a ruling class

[13] *Ibid.*, p. 53.
[14] *Ibid.*, pp. 65–66.

can also be revitalized by the incorporation of whole groups into the governing elite. Thus he observes that "the governing class is restored not only in numbers but — and that is the more important thing — in quality, by families rising from the lower classes. . . ." [15] In any event, the failure of the governing elite to remain receptive to new recruits representing developing "residues" (societal values) precipitates revolution.[16] Pareto also emphasized that the end of a cycle can be detected not only by the slowing down of the circulation of elites but also by the predominance of foxes over lions (manipulative skills over courage and strength) in the governing elite. The "shrinking from the use of force by the higher class simply allows the potential elites in the lower strata, who are prepared to use force, to develop and flourish. In the first stage of decline power is maintained by bargaining and concessions, and people are so deceived into thinking that that policy can be carried on indefinitely." [17] Hence in the conviction that "demagogic plutocracy" was a foreseen event, Pareto's mammoth study on social equilibrium closes on a note of despair.

II

Persistent Mosca won his fight, at least in the eyes of history, with his bitter rival, Pareto. For in adding six chapters to his major opus years after it was "finished," Mosca ended on a note of resolution, not despair. He had at last an answer to the basic question: how can political science contribute to the elimination of revolutions "which from time to time, interrupt the course of civilization and thrust peoples that have won glorious places in history back into barbarism . . ." [18]? The key to the problem, of course, was to maintain an open elite system, providing "a slow and continuous modification of the ruling classes," reflecting the

[15] *Mind and Society*, vol. III, p. 1430, quoted in T. B. Bottomore, *Elites and Society* (London, 1964), p. 42.

[16] In Pareto's words, "Revolution comes about through accumulation in the higher strata of society of decadent elements no longer possessing the residues suitable for keeping them in power, and shrinking from the use of force" (#2057).

[17] *Ibid.*, #2059.

[18] *The Ruling Class*, pp. 457–58.

changing social forces of the time.[19] Mosca and Pareto had long been aware of the validity of this principle, but how could a ruling class be prevented from committing suicide? "A political organism, a nation, a civilization," declared Mosca, "can, literally speaking, be *immortal,* provided it learns how to *transform itself continually without falling apart.*" [20]

In finally recognizing the utility of the elective and representative institutions, Mosca was well on the way to reconciling elitist and democratic principles, and, at the same time, solving the problem that had plagued him so many years. The incorporation of these institutions within the political system, Mosca argued, was essential not only to exercise reciprocal control and restraint among elite groups, but equally important, to provide institutional means to assure an opportunity for new elites representing diverse forces in society to rise to positions of power. The principles embodied in free elections, political equality and majority rule, were still regarded by Mosca as myths but only in the sense that their full exercise by the people could never result in their seizing power from the elite. But they were important in assuring an open ruling class. In Mosca's words:

> To be sure, majority government and absolute political equality, two of the mottos that the century inscribed on its banners, were not achieved, because they could not be achieved, and the same may be said of fraternity. But the ranks of the ruling classes have been held open. The barriers that kept individuals of the lower classes from entering the higher have been either removed or lowered, and the development of the old absolutist state into the modern representative state has made it possible for almost all political forces, almost all social values, to participate in the political management of society.[21]

Mosca was fully aware of the interrelationship of political organization and social forces. In contrast to the founding fathers, he was sure that political institutions are ineffectual in performing their task unless they in fact represent the "organized expression of a social influence and a social authority that has some standing

19 *Ibid.,* p. 462.
20 Mosca's emphasis, *ibid.*
21 *Ibid.,* p. 474.

in the community." [22] An effective equilibrium among political institutions is therefore dependent upon the balance of social forces which sustain them. On the other hand, Mosca held that political institutions provide an essential medium for political expression and representation, the absence or malfunctioning of which would endanger the proper circulation of elites. Thus political organization and form become, after all, of crucial importance to Mosca's theory.

But what is of greater significance is the radical shift in his concept of the ruling class and its relationship to the masses. The ruling class is no longer an organized cohesive minority obeying a single impulse; instead it consists of organized minorities, obeying diffuse and conflicting impulses. The dictum on the universality of the role of unified elites is brushed aside to make room for the more liberal and, it should be noted, more empirically defensible concept of elite pluralism. He now speaks of the conflict within the ruling classes, especially between interests derived from popular suffrage and the "liberal principle" and those whose source of power is the bureaucracy and the aristocracy. [23] Moreover, the wide and diverse representation of political forces participating in the political process is bound to provide a greater degree of governmental sensitivity to the interests of the general public. In short, the emphasis shifts from manipulation and exploitation of the masses by the elite, to the limitation and control of elites within the ruling class by the alignment of differing political forces in separate and opposing political institutions. Only when "all political forces and capacities . . . make themselves felt in public life" and political institutions "exercise . . . reciprocal control and limitation . . . is the indispensable condition of liberty" assured. [24] Finally, although Mosca persisted in regarding political equality as a myth, he implicitly espoused it in the form of political opportunity, an equality that is an integral part of the open ruling class which he so strongly advocated. [25]

Despite these concessions, the democratic aspects of Mosca's

[22] *Ibid.*, p. 138.
[23] *Ibid.*, pp. 474–75, 487.
[24] *Ibid.*, p. 488.
[25] See note 20.

theory should not be exaggerated. For he remained essentially an elitist to the end. The world of politics, indeed the destiny of the nation, lay, he believed, in the hands of the ruling class. The masses counted for nothing more than a source for supplying the ruling class with talented and ambitious individuals. As long as these individuals were effectively assimilated in the ruling class, there was no need to fear political instability and, least of all, revolution. And the stability and vitality of the ruling class, not the plight of the common man, were the key to the continued assurance of man's liberty, of civilization itself. These beliefs were the core of Mosca's political thought and are clearly manifested in both the early and later chapters of *The Ruling Class*.

The democratic institutions that were incorporated in his later theory as necessary means to assure the continued openness of the ruling class could not but benefit the lower classes, especially those individuals from the ranks who rose to elite positions. But the idea of a dialogue on public policy within and among publics and between ordinary men and elites was completely foreign to Mosca. As he envisaged it, the concept of openness was intended not to encourage the communication of ideas and programs and the expression of demands but to promote the revitalization of the elite by encouraging men of vigor and talent to rise to the top.

In perceiving the insight underlying the apparent paradox that democratic methods prudently used can enhance the strength and stability of a ruling class, Mosca solved his problem. But before his theory could be successfully integrated within the context of modern democratic theory, the theory of democracy itself required radical revision — a revision which was destined to transform it from a theory based upon ideals relating to the dignity and worth of individual man to a political method, disassociated from any particular ideals or ultimate values. The principal revisionist was the eminent economist Joseph Schumpeter.

III

Shortly before the publication of Joseph Schumpeter's *Capitalism, Socialism, and Democracy* (1942), Carl Becker wrote, "Modern liberal-democracy is associated with an ideology which rests upon something more than the minimum assumptions essential to any democratic government. It rests upon a philosophy of universally valid ends and means. Its fundamental assumption is the worth and dignity and creative capacity of the individual, so that the chief aim of government is the maximum of individual self-direction, the chief means to that end, the minimum of compulsion by the state . . . means and ends are conjoined in the concept of freedom; freedom of thought, so that the truth may prevail; freedom of occupation, so that careers may be open to talent; freedom of self-government, so that no one may be compelled against his will." [26]

It was this concept of democracy — conceived of as ideology, comprising both means and ends — against which Schumpeter leveled his main attack. And he did so in his usual graceful and indirect manner by posing an imaginary situation.

> Let us transport ourselves into a hypothetical country that, in a democratic way, practices the persecution of Christians, the burning of witches, and the slaughtering of Jews. We should certainly not approve of these practices on the ground that they have been decided on according to the rules of democratic procedure. But the crucial question is: would we approve of the democratic constitution itself that produced such results in preference to a non-democratic one that would avoid them? [27]

He believes that it would be most reasonable for a democrat to answer this question in the negative, and that this should not come as a shock since "there are ultimate ideals and interests which the most ardent democrat will put above democracy. . . ." [28] And the reason for this, of course, is that "democracy is a political *method*, that is to say, a certain type of institutional arrangement for arriving at political . . . decisions and hence incapable of being an end in itself, irrespective of what decisions it will produce under given historical conditions." [29] The inference of Schumpeter is clear: an individual gives his uncompromising allegiance and loyalty to ideals and interests which he cherishes, and quali-

[26] *Modern Democracy* (New Haven, 1941), pp. 26–27.
[27] *Capitalism, Socialism, and Democracy* (London, 1961 edition), p. 242.
[28] *Ibid.*
[29] *Ibid.*

fied allegiance to a political method, such as democracy, which he expects will serve these ends. However, if democracy actually works contrary to expectation, he should not suffer great guilt feelings through turning his back upon it; for it would be less than rational to defend a political method that was jeopardizing an individual's ideals or interests.[30]

Thus by the reduction of democracy to a political method on the strength of what Schumpeter considered simple logic and common sense, the way became open to modifying and qualifying democracy in the interest, for example, of protecting liberty, without undue embarrassment and equivocation. It is quite different, in other words, to profess uncompromising loyalty to a political philosophy based upon the dignity and worth of man than to give allegiance to a political method that is *expected* to protect and strengthen individual liberty, justice, and the like. Without this masterful stroke on Schumpeter's part, it is doubtful that elitism and democracy could have developed as they have into a congenial and close relationship. For in the absence of his version of democratic theory, on-going democratic systems, which require little more of the great majority of people than to choose periodically between competing leaders, would be continually vulnerable to attack for failing to provide the political means and climate which stimulate and heighten the development of a free people. But such criticism is inappropriate, and misfires when applied to a political method that is committed to the achievement of no overriding objectives or ideals.

What is ironical, however, is that Schumpeter's famous hypothetical question was based upon a misconception of democratic procedure. His question is based on the fallacious assumption that "the persecution of Christians, the burning of witches, and the slaughtering of Jews" could be carried out "in a democratic way" and "according to the rules of democratic procedure." [31] Clearly any one of these actions would constitute a violation of democracy even when conceived solely as a method. Religious, racial, or group persecution of any sort is in conflict with the principles of freedom of discussion and association essen-

[30] *Ibid.*, pp. 242–43.
[31] See note 26.

tial to the operation of the majority rule principle. For if a minority is barred forcefully from becoming a majority, such action cannot be squared with the rules of democratic procedure. Thus Schumpeter posed a false dilemma: it is not a question of standing by one's loyalty to democracy when a minority is being brutalized; mob rule and majority tyranny are outrages against both democracy and individual liberty. Consequently, as formulated by Schumpeter, there is no question of divided loyalty between democratic means and liberal ends. Nevertheless, the intent of Schumpeter's thrust — that democracy, owing to its inherent nature, is constantly in danger of violation of its own principles — is unlikely to be lost for most readers.

Schumpeter substantially narrowed the meaning of democracy (even when conceived solely as a political method). Without undue difficulty, he showed that eighteenth-century ideas of "the common good" and "the will of the people" are myths; that it is absurd to believe that "the people" have rational views on every issue and that the function of their representatives is to carry out their views in the legislative chambers.[32] Instead of the concept "government by the people," he proposed "government approved by the people."[33] Thus the democratic method is defined as "that institutional arrangement for arriving at political decisions in which individuals acquire the power to decide by means of a competitive struggle for the people's vote."[34]

On the question of what constitutes sufficient breadth of the franchise to meet democratic requirements, he is highly permissive. He suggests that any limitation of the right to vote is a reasonable one if it is not "without absurdity or insincerity."[35] Under this criterion he sees no objection if a nation discriminates on the basis of property, race, sex, or religion.[36] In viewing fitness to vote as a matter of opinion, he believes it is understandable that "a race-conscious nation may associate fitness with racial considerations."[37] Prohibition on such grounds should not therefore be

[32] *Ibid.*, p. 269.
[33] *Ibid.*, p. 246.
[34] *Ibid.*, p. 269.
[35] *Ibid.*, p. 244.
[36] *Ibid.*, pp. 244–45.
[37] *Ibid.*, p. 244.

considered undemocratic; such matters, he believed, should be left for "every populus" to decide for itself.

In regard to the requirements of political leadership in a democracy, Schumpeter's standards become somewhat exclusive. Viewing the English aristocracy as a model, he believed that the existence of leaders of high caliber in a nation is dependent upon a social stratum which "is neither too exclusive nor too easily accessible for the outsider" and is sufficiently strong to assimilate individuals from lower classes who make the grade.[38] His rigidity in this respect is understandable since his theory of democracy, as reflected in his definition of the concept, "leaves all the room we may wish to have for a proper recognition of the vital facts of leadership." [39] And if elites are to exercise their rightful power effectively, the people must understand that they cannot take political action between elections. Even "bombarding" representatives with letters and telegrams, Schumpeter argued, ought to be banned.[40]

His concept of democracy was aptly summarized in one sentence: "Democracy means only that the people have the opportunity of accepting or refusing the men who are to rule them." [41] Mosca's theory of a stable and open political system ruled by elites fits nicely in the democratic frame reconstructed by Joseph Schumpeter.

IV

In following Schumpeter's lead, contemporary theorists generally agree that "democracy has no overriding purpose to promote"; [42] that dispensing with the vagueness of goals, values, and purposes, democracy, conceived as "a method for choosing leaders or rulers," [43] is subject to a more promising, scientific definition, analogous to economic concepts. As Henry Mayo points

---

[38] *Ibid.*, p. 291.

[39] *Ibid.*, p. 270.

[40] *Ibid.*, p. 295.

[41] *Ibid.*, p. 285.

[42] H. B. Mayo, *An Introduction to Democratic Theory* (New York, 1960), p. 248.

[43] H. B. Mayo, "How Can We Justify Democracy?" *American Political Science Review* (1962), p. 557.

out, "Economic systems are not distinguishable by what goods and services are produced, and economic analysis never approaches them from that direction . . . it does not start with philosophic discussions on the content of particular decisions, or the ideal standard of living." [44] Thus in this vein, Schumpeter has served political science well by suggesting that it follow the approach used so effectively in its sister discipline. The argument, however, cannot be pushed too far, since, as Galbraith has observed, we must now be concerned in economics not only with the old problem of maintaining a full utilization of human and economic resources, but in addition, with the problem of providing a more socially justifiable balance between the public and private sector of the economy. Hence the purpose of economic activity and — Mayo's point notwithstanding — even the issue as to what constitutes "the ideal standard of living" cannot but be germane to economics. Ironically, at the very time that the economists are being pushed to consider more closely the purposes and aims of economic activity, the political scientists are moving in the opposite direction, emulating economic science of a decade or two ago.

Schumpeter's view of democracy is also receptive to contemporary theorists who have proclaimed an "end of ideology." [45] If American democracy is to remain an open society, it must, in Daniel Boorstin's words, remain free of "the Un-American demand for a philosophy of democracy," [46] and unlike other nations who "have filled their sanctuaries with ideological idols," we must keep our sanctum empty.[47] Democracy therefore must remain above all ideologies, confining itself to reaching decisions on concrete issues while at the same time keeping the future open. Put aptly by Thomas Thorson, the hallmark of a democratic system must perpetually be: "Do not block the possibility of change with respect to social goals." [48]

It is unlikely that any democrat would quarrel with this dic-

[44] *An Introduction to Democratic Theory*, p. 33.
[45] Daniel Bell's phrase. See his *The End of Ideology* (Glencoe, Ill., 1960).
[46] *The Genius of American Politics* (paperback edition, Chicago, 1962), p. 184.
[47] *Ibid.*, p. 170.
[48] *The Logic of Democracy* (New York, 1962), p. 139.

tum. However, it must be realized that if it is viewed politically rather than philosophically, strict observance is impossible. For, in the first place, any decision which results in changing a social goal is likely to block any serious reconsideration of it in the future. The issues of slavery, progressive income tax, trade unionism, and social security, for example, were all fervently fought out in the arena of American politics in past years, yet it is doubtful that any one of them is subject to serious reconsideration now or will be in the future. Issues which are once "settled" tend to develop politically vested interests which immunize them from future challenge. Secondly, any major change in political policy and attitude affects the course of future change; the rise of the welfare state generates further experimentation with and acceptability of state intervention in areas heretofore considered beyond the legitimate sphere of government responsibility. It is not a likely possibility that in the name of rugged individualism and free enterprise the federal government will revert to a pre-Keynesian policy by staying its hand and allowing the business cycle to take its natural course.

The "openness" of a society is thus only meaningful within the context of its present development. It is bound politically not only by substantive decisions of the past, which have helped shape the present, but also by the procedures and principles governing the decision-making process at any given time.[49] One can legitimately argue, as Schumpeter did, that democracy is a method bound neither to interests nor to ideals; nevertheless, he could hardly argue that his concept of the democratic method — or indeed any other — would not have a substantial influence both on the type of issues which would be considered and on the actual decisions reached.

The crucial question therefore is not whether the democratic method is open in a particular interpretation, but for whom it is open, and for what purpose. Not to answer this question explicitly on the grounds that it would somehow close the system is to assume mistakenly that an open system is precluded from

[49] Peter Bachrach and Morton Baratz, "Decisions and Nondecisions: An Analytical Framework," *American Political Science Review* (vol. 57, 1963), pp. 641–42.

dedication to an ideal. If this were the case, then the classical democratic position that the maximization of the self-development of every individual is the paramount objective of democracy would constitute a basic contradiction. Surely, this has not been shown to be the case. In fact, notwithstanding the realist's position, it is still arguable whether providing the political method with an end toward which society can strive enhances rather than detracts from the openness of the system.

On the other hand, to insist that democracy is simply a political method, devoid of a dominant purpose, is to leave the theorist in the position of saying that democracy is that political system which actually exists in various countries, such as the United States, Britain, Canada, and the like.[50] The fundamental disadvantage of this criterion is that it gives the theorist no basis for judging whether the system is becoming more democratic or more elitist in nature. He can attempt to overcome this difficulty by comparing the development of democracy with on-going totalitarian systems. This criterion is indeed used by leading contemporary theorists.[51] For example, in defense of democracy in its present form, Raymond Aron points out that the crucial difference between "a society of the Soviet type and one of the Western type is that the former has a unified elite and the latter a divided elite. . . ." [52] Subscribing to the same approach, Louis Hartz argues that there is no crisis of democracy; that by any earthly standards it is the best system yet devised. Realizing this hard fact, we

[50] Robert Dahl, *Modern Political Analysis* (Englewood Cliffs, N.J., 1963), p. 73.

[51] See Robert Dahl, *A Preface to Democratic Theory* (Chicago, 1956), pp. 132–33; John Plamenatz, "Electoral Studies and Democratic Theory," *Political Studies* (1958), pp. 1–9; Raymond Aron, "Social Structure and the Ruling Class," *The British Journal of Sociology* (no. 1, March, 1950), pp. 1–17; *Ibid.* (no. 2, June, 1950), pp. 126–44; G. Sartori, *op. cit.*, p. 116; and Louis Hartz, in *Power and Civilization.*

[52] *Op. cit.*, no. 1, p. 10. Offhand it appears rather bleak to regard the fundamental difference between totalitarianism and democracy in terms of the role of elites in each system rather than the role of the people. Does this mean that we are content, in the name of reality, that the general public in a democracy, as in a totalitarian country, is passive and that what role it does play is secondary? Can a viable democratic theory be built on this premise?

should not be disillusioned because we have not lived up to the myths embodied in the eighteenth-century model of democracy. He concludes on the optimistic note that "in the argument with Communism we have more to hope from an inexorable disenchantment on its part than from an impossible attempt to recapture the Eighteenth Century on our part." [53] Carrying Hartz's argument a step further, if the rate of disillusionment in the Soviet Union is indeed greater than ours, and their system as a result collapses, what criterion will we then have for judging our system? Perhaps the greater danger is that the Soviet system will not collapse, leaving us perpetually tied to a totalitarian standard against which to appraise the performance of our own system. As long as this line of reasoning persists, the fate of democracy rests with the liberalization, not the deterioration, of the Soviet system.

An alternative approach is to appraise the political method in terms of its various operating principles, such as political equality, freedom of discussion, accountability of leaders to the electorate, and the like. The difficulty here, however, is that these principles, as we will discover, are open to a wide range of interpretations. In the absence of a broader criterion relating to the purpose of democracy, how can an intelligent dialogue on the conflicting interpretations of these principles be possible? Moreover, without such a criterion, is not the theorist likely to interpret these principles exclusively by the realistic standard which measures the soundness of an interpretation according to the degree to which it mirrors the demonstrable facts relating to the political system at a given time? For example, if the present trend towards an increase in elite power continues, will not the theorist be inclined to bend and adjust these principles to meet changing conditions, even though the trend is approaching the point of jeopardizing the democratic method? Judged by recent democratic theory, it is likely that he will.

Thus we have the legacy of Joseph Schumpeter. And it is a legacy embraced by an age disenchanted with the common man, and an age, consequently, that is receptive to a more qualified and moderate version of democracy.

[53] *Op. cit.*, p. 379.

3
The revolt
from the masses

T HE TENSION between liberalism and democracy
— between freedom to be left alone and freedom to participate in
decisions which affect oneself and one's community — is evident
among contemporary liberals.[1] Until recently the works of de
Tocqueville were regarded as historically "dated." Today his
thesis on the perverse impact of equalitarianism upon a free society
is seriously studied by all students of democracy.[2]

In the past, the democratic theorists experienced little difficulty

[1] For an excellent paper on the theoretical development and inherent conflict between these two liberties, see Isaiah Berlin, *Two Concepts of Liberty*
(Clarendon Press, Oxford, 1958).

[2] Bernard Crick, a British political scientist, criticized his American colleagues for not contemplating and taking to heart de Tocqueville's message.
Today his barb could not have been further from the mark. For I do not
believe that there is any theorist who is more widely read and taken to
heart — with the possible exception of the authors of the *Federalist Papers* —
than de Tocqueville. In sharp contrast with the democratic theorists whom
Crick studied, such as Charles Merriam and T. V. Smith, contemporary
American theorists, as I hope this study makes clear, are very much indeed
attuned to de Tocqueville's thought. Crick's book is *American Science of
Politics* (London, 1956). See especially pp. 242–43.

in reconciling democracy and liberalism. For in the eighteenth and nineteenth centuries, the threat of tyranny emanated primarily from the ruling elites, from corrupt and decadent monarchies, and from power-hungry, arbitrary, and unrepresentative parliaments.[3] Jefferson's support for a constitutional system of checks and balances was not prompted, as it was in the *Federalist Papers*, by fear of majority tyranny of the people, but by fear of minority tyranny of the ruling elite. For the same reason, he insisted upon a Bill of Rights, not as a shield against majority tyranny, but to protect the principle of majority rule.[4] To be sure, people were corruptible, but it was assumed that the source of corruption was faulty political, economic, and social institutions.

To free man from the corrupting forces of society was imperative if the majority was to fulfill its responsibility of performing the task as guardian of society's freedom. Thus what was called for was more, not less, democracy. This entailed not only extending the right of the franchise, but also, as neo-liberals such as Hobhouse were later to advocate, utilizing government to provide a minimum standard of living for all and the protection of the individual from the arbitrary wielding of power by nongovernmental groups and organizations.

In the course of the evolution of democratic government during the nineteenth century and the first thirty-five years of the twentieth, democrats generally believed that the continued extension and growth of democracy was the best assurance of the preservation of constitutional liberalism. From the outset, the belief was grounded on the assumption that the common man inherently was capable of good judgment and that his occasional manifestations of irrationality and hostility toward the democratic process were symptomatic of a malfunctioning society.[5]

[3] See R. R. Palmer, *The Age of Democratic Revolution* (Princeton, 1959), especially Chapters IV and VI.

[4] Contrary to Leonard Levy's thesis, Jefferson's advocacy of political libel trials by the states is not inconsistent with his attachment to the Bill of Rights. For Levy's thesis, see *Jefferson and Civil Liberties: The Darker Side* (Cambridge, Mass., 1963).

[5] Accepting the challenge of democracy, American social scientists, as Bernard Crick admirably shows, concentrated upon building a science that would provide the techniques and instrumentalities to improve the system,

Events reaffirmed the faith of the liberal democrat. Especially in England and America, it was the great mass of people, first the middle and then the working classes, who were the major force in extending democracy and constitutional liberties. In exerting continuous pressure for the expansion of the franchise, they were instrumental in building the foundations of modern democratic constitutionalism — the two party system. And if the working classes had not waged a long and bitter struggle for essential economic and social reform, it is doubtful that even a remnant of constitutionalism would have survived in the world today.[6] Freedom of speech, crucial as an instrument of majorities in their struggle for reform, appeared not only to safeguard civil liberties but to broaden and vitalize them. Moreover, it appeared equally true that Jefferson was basically right: that in the last analysis, it is the mass of the people, not the elite, who are the true guardians of liberty.

Even the rise of totalitarianism in Italy and Germany, and the stark realization of its existence in the Soviet Union, did not noticeably dampen democratic beliefs. In fact, it made some democrats more militant. For example, on the eve of World War II, Carl Becker argued that the proper and effective retort to fascist and Communist challenge was widespread internal economic and social reform. He was convinced that the survival of democracy depended upon the rectification of the "flagrant inequality of possessions and of opportunity now existing in democratic societies." [7] Not to adopt effective means to achieve this objective, he observed, would be to invite the common man to turn to another system which promised a tolerable life.[8] Becker, who was the epitome of Aristotle's moderate man, could see no effective means

---

to clear away the barriers to the full realization of the political system. The result of this ambitious effort unfortunately led, in large part, to the sterility of "scientism," and more importantly, to discouraging the development of speculative and critical political thought. See note 2 above for Crick's book.

[6] For example, in France where reform was abortive, the workers became alienated from the system, as reflected in their widespread support of the Communist party. See Herbert Tint, *The Decline of French Patriotism — 1870–1940* (London, 1964).

[7] *Modern Democracy* (New Haven, 1941), p. 67.

[8] *Ibid.*, p. 7.

for safeguarding the democratic process other than to democratize society at least to the point where all groups within its bounds could reasonably be expected to be attached to it. Also adhering to this thesis, Max Lerner argued [9] that the Weimar Republic fell not because of an overzealous majority but because of political stalemate, the inability of the government to act decisively in the interests of the majority of the people.[10] He recognized the dangers inherent in majority rule, but he regarded the irresponsible actions of elites upon the body politic as a greater danger. He called for the rise of a militant democracy to reassert itself against the "aristocracy of wealth and the insolence of power." [11] Like Becker he saw no way to safeguard civil liberties other than by effectively organizing majority will in support of vigorous and dynamic government. "I can say only that the political job of our time must be the heroic effect of making our society as safe as possible for the majority principle." [12]

With the onslaught of postwar reaction and the rise of McCarthyism in America, the democratic faith in the common man, if not shattered, was subjected to serious doubt. The widespread alliance between workingmen and the Communist parties in France and Italy, and trade union support of Perón in Argentina and Salazar in Portugal could be discounted to an extent in terms of Becker's and Lerner's thesis, but the persistent threat to freedom from these quarters was a new and frightening phenomenon. For unlike the days of the Alien and Sedition Acts and the Palmer raids, McCarthy was not vigorously opposed by any sector in the society and had the tacit approval, if not the active support, of an uncomfortably large number of people from all strata of society.[13] What was particularly baffling was that the McCarthyite reaction occurred and persisted during a period of relative affluence. On hindsight, it appears that affluence is conducive to reaction for

[9] *It Is Later Than You Think* (New York, 1943).

[10] This interpretation is now generally accepted by scholars. See, for example, Alan Bullock, *Hitler: A Study in Tyranny* (London, 1954), pp. 253–55.

[11] Lerner, *op. cit.*, p. 118.

[12] *Ibid.*, p. 111.

[13] See Talcott Parsons, "Social Strains in America," in Daniel Bell (ed.), *The New American Right* (New York, 1955).

two reasons: first, it is an ideal setting for those suffering from the social tensions of an acquisitive society to vent their anxieties and bewilderment in political movements of the right.[14] Secondly, it tends to dry up political protest from the left; the labor movement becomes nonmilitant and businesslike; intellectuals situated in lucrative and prestigious posts lose their taste for social criticism.

Such an explanation, however, does not, in the eyes of either liberal or radical democrats, alter their disillusionment about the common man. He turns out, after all, not to be attached to the cause of liberty, fraternity, or, indeed, equality;[15] and when his socioeconomic interests are not at stake, he may become indifferent toward the fate of freedom itself. It is feared that, given the opportunity, he is more inclined to support than oppose the demagogue's attack against freedom.

This is the chief reason, I suggest, for the radical shift in democratic thought in the postwar period. The nature of this shift is illustrated most clearly in Max Lerner's writings. For example, in his ambitious book, *America as Civilization* (1957), Lerner seems more concerned with defending than with reforming the American political system; the dangers of political stalemate and of minority rule are pushed aside in favor of praise for the "widespread diffusion of power and the talent for equilibrium [that the American system] has shown."[16] A similar shift, although considerably less marked, is also reflected in the writings of Franz Neuman during the last few years of his life. He too retreated from pressing for a further democratization of society to a defense of existing democratic systems. And to defend the system, he did not turn to the proletarian but "to the scholars, teachers, intellectuals and artists."[17] Liberals generally became disinclined

[14] See Parsons, note 12.

[15] See Robert Lane, "Fear of Equality," *American Political Science Review* (vol. 53, 1959), pp. 35–51; and Seymour Lipset, "Working Class Authoritarianism," in his *Political Man* (Glencoe, Ill., 1960).

[16] *America as Civilization* (New York, 1957), p. 399.

[17] *The Democratic and the Authoritarian State* (New York, 1957), p. 212. For an excellent critique of Neuman, see David Kettler "Dilemma of Radicalism," *Dissent*, August, 1957, p. 390. Karl Mannheim became aware of the danger of mass support of totalitarianism considerably earlier than most radicals, including Lerner and Neuman. In *Man and Society in the Age of*

toward the traditional criticism of American institutions voiced by Parrington, Beard, and J. Allen Smith, and began to emphasize the dangers of majority tyranny and extol the virtues of judicial review, checks and balances, and the pluralist system, characterized by compromise and government by consensus. The authority of social science has in recent years increasingly supported this position.

The findings of public opinion and personality research documented the theorists' suspicion that the great majority of people have a surprisingly weak commitment to democratic values. Samuel Stouffer's study on the attitude of Americans toward civil liberties showed that the rank and file of organizations are less attached than leaders to the principles of civil liberties and democratic procedures.[18] Moreover, his study showed that leaders from conservative organizations, such as the Daughters of the American Revolution, were more permissive toward the rights of others than the rank and file of liberal organizations, such as trade unions.[19] In his article "Working Class Authoritarianism," Seymour Lipset reached the conclusion, based upon findings of numerous studies, that the lower strata are relatively more authoritarian than either the middle or upper classes.[20] The authori-

---

Reconstruction (London, 1940) he stated, "The source of our criticism consists neither in the snobbish condemnation of the masses which is so widespread nowadays, nor in cheap grumbling about the principles of liberalism and democracy. The ultimate drive is rather the wish to make an appeal to those to whom freedom and justice are still ultimate values, to think about the proper means to secure them . . ." (p. 106).

For Mannheim the appeal must be made to the intellectual elite, who, he believed, are committed to freedom, and capable, through the utilization of social techniques and planning, to lead a directionless mass society to the safety of an ordered constitutional democracy. In the absence of a strong elite, dedicated to a free society, the continued drift of society would inevitably lead to dictatorship. In his later writings, such as *Diagnosis of Our Times* (London, 1943), he became less elitist and more democratically inclined, although he never was convincing as to how planners were to be democratically controlled. See *Freedom, Power, and Democratic Planning* (New York, 1950).

[18] *Communism, Conformity and Civil Liberties* (New York, 1955).

[19] *Ibid.*, pp. 29–42.

[20] In his *Political Man, op. cit.*, p. 101.

tarian predispositions of the lower classes, he believes, are caused chiefly by social isolation and lack of sufficient exposure to and participation in either political or voluntary organizations.[21] Lipset cautions the reader, however, that the latent authoritarianism of the working classes does not necessarily constitute a threat to the democratic system. A combination of factors would have to exist for this force to become overt.[22] Nevertheless, the major thrust of his argument is that, all other things being equal, the working classes are the major threat to freedom.[23]

II

With the disenchantment with the common man, the classical view of the elite-mass relationship has become reversed: it is the common man, not the elite, who is chiefly suspected of endangering freedom, and it is the elite, not the common man, who is looked upon as the chief guardian of the system. The revolt from the masses has led to a second shift in theory: the emphasis is no longer upon extending or strengthening democracy, but upon stabilizing the established system. The focus, in short, is upon protecting liberalism from the excesses of democracy rather than upon utilizing liberal means to progress toward the realization of democratic ideals. Political equilibrium is the fundamental value of the new theory. Thus the political passivity of the great majority of the people is not regarded as an element of democratic malfunctioning, but on the contrary, as a necessary condition for allowing the creative functioning of the elite. The empirical and normative aspects of the theory supplement each other: empirically we find that the masses are relatively unreliable but as a rule passive, and the elites relatively reliable and dominant in making the important decisions for society. The on-going system tends to be the desired system.

These observations, I believe, are well reflected in the currently developing theory of democratic elitism. In the remainder of this chapter and in the next, I plan to trace this development by

[21] *Ibid.*, p. 109.

[22] *Ibid.*, p. 129.

[23] For criticism of his thesis on methodological and substantive grounds, see S. M. Miller and Frank Riessman, "Working Class Authoritarianism: A Critique of Lipset," *British Journal of Sociology* (vol. 12, 1961), pp. 263–81.

analyzing the thought of various theorists who have contributed to it.

In one of the comparatively early comprehensive studies of voting behavior, a team of Columbia University sociologists, led by Bernard Berelson, found that, contrary to the assumptions underlying classical democratic theory, a great number of people are lacking in motivation, interest, and knowledge concerning politics and political issues. An older tradition of democratic theory would have concluded from this that the system wasn't working right, or that if it was, it wasn't a democratic system by the standards of democratic theory. Undaunted by these findings, the authors set out to show in their concluding chapter not only that the political attributes of the electorate failed to jeopardize the democratic system but that they were indeed essential to it; that the defect lay not in the deficiencies of the voters but in classical theory. The fact that the democratic system in the United States had survived and grown suggested to them that "where the classic theory is defective is in its concentration on the *individual* citizen." [24] From the standpoint of the "requirements for the survival of the total democratic system," [25] the authors show, for example, that nonvoters (roughly forty percent) and marginal voters — those who have least interest, and owing to conflicting social pressures, are erratic and inconsistent in their beliefs — provide the flexibility required of the system. Thus "an individual 'inadequacy' provides a positive service for the system." [26] Similarly, a relatively low commitment to party and political beliefs by those who do not participate in political life is conducive to compromise and stability. The heterogeneous nature of the electorate produces political pluralism which "makes for enough consensus to hold the system together and enough cleavage to make it move." [27]

[24] Bernard Berelson, *et al., Voting* (Chicago, 1954), p. 312.

[25] *Ibid.,* p. 322.

[26] *Ibid.,* p. 316.

[27] *Ibid.,* p. 318. Along the same lines, recent studies have shown that citizens who tend to have authoritarian predispositions are also low in political participation, and those who are most committed to democratic values tend to be the leaders and influentials of society. For summary discussion of these studies, see Fred I. Greenstein, *The American Party System and the American People* (Englewood Cliffs, N.J., 1963), pp. 18–34.

To depart from classical theory, as Berelson and his colleagues did, by focusing on the requirements of the democratic system, instead of on the political behavior of the individual, appears sound. It is suggestive of the scientist's approach to the living organism; the criterion for determining whether a particular unit of the organism is healthy or unhealthy is judged primarily in terms of whether it adequately contributes to the well-being of the organism as a whole. And it is a reasonable assumption that if the total organism is functioning normally, the individual parts of the organism are in good health. It would appear that the analogy applies to the body politic; if the individual units of the political system contribute to its well-being, it stands to reason that the system is in good health and will thrive. Conversely, it would seem reasonable to assume that a healthy, thriving system adequately provides for the well-being of its various parts.

The analogy breaks down, however, in two respects. In the first place, unlike a physical organism, the body politic is not, at least for a democrat, an end in itself, though the authors of the study under discussion come dangerously close to assuming this to be the case. Secondly, the implicit assumption that an apparently thriving democratic system is bound to provide a wide degree of freedom to its citizens is not necessarily true. Put differently, the issue comes down to whether there is a harmony of interest between an on-going democratic system and those who sustain it. The Athenian democratic polis thrived, but as Aristotle made clear, it depended upon the stable institution of slavery. The young American republic was not dependent upon such an institution, but for decades its democratic institutions grew and thrived despite the existence of slavery. In a less dramatic fashion, we have recently discovered that a democratic system can function well despite the fact, and with little public awareness, that one out of every five persons suffers from dire poverty and, in President Johnson's words, is "without hope." It is largely this group of people which supplies the nonvoters and marginal voters whom Berelson and his colleagues regard as essential to the required flexibility of a democratic system. If it is true that their " 'inadequacy' provides a positive service for the society," [28] does this mean that a rehabilitation of this large group will endanger the stability of the political system?

I am not arguing that the authors were in error in focusing on the requirements for sustaining a functioning political system rather than on the individual voter. But I am saying that they were in error in implying that because a political system is a viable and stable one, it is therefore also adequately contributing to the growth and well-being of ordinary men and women who live under it.

III

With considerably more sophistication and depth, the British political scientist John Plamenatz also attempted to square the recent findings of electoral studies and democratic theory.[29] His analysis is significant, especially for our purposes, since it is an intelligent statement of moderate democratic elitism.

Plamenatz concedes at the outset that the role of the electorate in mass society is primarily passive. But he argues that it does not follow that because the voter is passive – his primary function consisting of making a cross on a piece of paper – he is therefore manipulated. He is not manipulated because he has a choice between or among competing elites who are politically active, articulate, and as Plamenatz emphasizes, "who *between them* run the whole life of the community." [30] It is the betweenness which of course saves the day; in their debate and struggle between themselves, they present articulately and forcefully the alternative positions on pressing issues of the day. Without them, "there would be nothing worth calling public opinion; and in a democracy it is their business to make it without being able to decide what it shall be." [31] There is no manipulation, in short, as long as there is rule by elites, not by an elite.

To a large part Plamenatz discounts the significance of the pollsters' findings that the vast majority of voters tend to be ir-

[28] Berelson, *op. cit.*, p. 316.
[29] "Electoral Studies and Democratic Theory," *Political Studies* (no. 6, 1958), pp. 1–9.
[30] *Ibid.*, p. 5. His italics.
[31] *Ibid.*, p. 5.

rational and inarticulate on public issues. For he argues that a wise political choice is not necessarily contingent upon the capacity to reason in a logical and articulate fashion. "A choice is reasonable, not because the chooser, when challenged, can give a satisfactory explanation of why he made it, but because, if he could give an explanation, it would be satisfactory." [32] However, Plamenatz's defense of the common man's ability to make a wise choice is more or less limited to his choosing between rival political parties. It is similar to Edmund Burke's prudent insight that man should follow the dictates of his prejudice, which reflect the mores and customs of his society, rather than follow the dictates of abstract reasoning. Plamenatz observes that a person who votes for "party-image" is probably acting more reasonably than if "he votes because of what he thinks about the Middle East." [33] Thus, although democracy assigns the voter a basically passive role, there is no convincing reason to conclude — the findings of the electoral studies notwithstanding — that he cannot be counted on to perform the task adequately.

In the interval between elections, Plamenatz continues, pressure groups are operative, on the one hand, in preventing any one elite group from overreaching its legitimate bounds and, on the other, in representing vigorously and effectively the interests of the people. "The voice of the people," he states, "is heard everlastingly, between elections much more even than at them, through these [elite] spokesmen; and their demands are not vague but precise." [34] In concluding, he points out that the key to a continuing and healthy political pluralism, in which both the freedom and interests of the people are protected and served, is free periodic elections. They are essential to assure that elected leaders are legitimately in positions of power in accord with the will of the majority of the electorate.

Plamenatz's thesis is open to criticism on several grounds. First, it is doubtful whether the majority of people in any pluralist society are organized in pressure groups which effectively represent them between elections. It is not the case in America, which

[32] *Ibid.*, p. 8.
[33] *Ibid.*
[34] *Ibid.*, p. 9.

is a political model of a pressure group society. The data indicate that a relatively small minority of laborers, farmers, women, Negroes, and other lower and lower middle class persons are members of any organized interest group.[35] Commenting on the significance of these findings, E. E. Schattschneider declared: "The flaw in the pluralist heaven is that the heavenly chorus sings with a strong upperclass accent. Probably about 90 per cent of the people cannot get into the pressure system." [36] Secondly, Plamenatz's view that when the people are reasonably organized their demands are heard and respected is somewhat doubtful in light of our knowledge of the veto power of entrenched interests. The political implications of a system which is constantly in danger of stalemate, or, at best, government by consensus, are ignored.[37] Thirdly, there is considerable doubt about the validity of the assumption that elites are mutually restrained by competitive interaction among themselves. For example, the study of New York [38] by Sayre and Kaufman indicates that this is not the case, at least on the local political level; that instead, each elite tends to dominate in its own sphere of activity and to encounter little if any interference or concern from other elites. A pluralism of elites does not necessarily produce a competitive situation among elites.

Putting aside this line of criticism, can it be said that Plamenatz has successfully bridged the gap between the findings of the electoral studies and democratic theory? To be more precise, if we assume that the interests of ordinary men and women are protected and represented by the pluralist system, as Plamenatz contends, does the system meet the requirements of democratic theory?

One important requirement of democracy is that the people's interests be fulfilled. But this raises the question of the democratic

[35] See E. E. Schattschneider, *The Semisovereign People* (New York, 1960), pp. 20–41; Greenstein, *op. cit.*, p. 11; and A. Campbell, *The American Voter* (New York, 1960), p. 91.

[36] *Semisovereign People*, p. 35.

[37] See James Burns, *The Deadlock of Democracy* (Englewood Cliffs, N.J., 1963); and Stephen Bailey, *Congress Makes a Law* (New York, 1950).

[38] W. Sayre and Herbert Kaufmann, *Governing New York* (New York, 1959), pp. 719–20.

meaning of the concept of interest. On the basis of his thesis, it is clear that Plamenatz conceives of interest in terms of demands; that a man's political interests are met when his agent, such as his elected representative or the spokesman of his pressure group, is successful in meeting his demands. Undeniably this is an important part of the concept. And, significantly, it is that part which has some likelihood of being fulfilled by dint of a minimal expenditure of energy, time, and money by the individual; for, as Plamenatz would have it, by striking an X on a piece of paper every few years and paying annual fees to a pressure group whose policies are usually decided and carried out by men whom he probably neither knows nor has ever seen – an individual has a reasonable chance of having his political interests met. His concept of interest is nicely in harmony with the passivity of the people and the creative role of the elite.

There is, however, another aspect of the concept of interest which can also be said to be democratically important. It is interest not in the form of gains in material well-being, power, or status; but it is rather in personal satisfaction and growth attained from active engagement in the political process. It is interest conceived in terms of political means rather than political ends. Each complements the other and each is equally important in meeting the requirements of a healthy democracy. The young man rebels against his father's acting for him in his own best interest, not only because his father might not in fact know the son's best interest, but also because the son's dignity, his need to act for himself, is at stake. Similarly, it would seem reasonable to assume that the full development of the personalities of adult men and women requires the opportunity and challenge to participate in public life beyond the ballot box and dues collection.

Perhaps the realization of political-interest-as-means for a more extensive group than elites is impossible in modern industrial societies. I do not believe that this is the case. It is unlikely, however, that the problem will receive serious attention as long as the theory of democratic elitism continues to be widely accepted by both scholars and the public. For there is little reason to undertake serious analysis of this problem if we accept the assurances of Plamenatz and other leading political theorists that the essential requirements of democracy are, under present conditions, fulfilled in practice. For example, in the course of his argument, Plamenatz points out that Michels' pessimistic conclusion regarding the inevitable tendency of organizations to become oligarchic need not really trouble the democrat, since, as in the case of the political party, oligarchic organizations play a vital nonoligarchical role in a pluralist competitive society.[39] In focusing on the requirements of the system, the fate of a large number of individuals who are enmeshed in giant oligarchic hierarchies is ignored.[40] Again, as in the case of the Berelson study, we see that there is not necessarily a harmony of interest between the requirements for a stable democratic system, as conceived by contemporary theorists, and the requirements for free men. Ironically, most theorists are quite aware of the disharmony when it is put in the familiar formula regarding the tensions between democracy and liberalism. But the lesson seems to be forgotten when the tensions are between elitism and democracy.

IV

In his treatise *Democratic Theory*,[41] Giovanni Sartori warns: "Distrust and fear of elites is an anachronism that blinds us to the problem of the future." Democracy must no longer be on guard against aristocracy when the more formidable danger springs from the opposite direction — mediocrity. "What we have to fear then," continues Sartori, "is that democracy — as in the myth of Saturn — may destroy its own leaders, thereby creating the conditions for their replacement by undemocratic counterelites." [42] In the tradition of Mosca and Pareto, he does not fear a

[39] "Electoral Studies and Democratic Theory," *op. cit.*, pp. 1–9; for Robert Michels' argument, see *Political Parties* (Free Press, 1949), especially pp. 365–408.

[40] Kariel observed: "The voluntary organizations or associations which the early theorists of pluralism relied upon to sustain the individual against a unified omnipotent government, have themselves become oligarchically governed hierarchies." *The Decline of American Pluralism* (Stanford, California, 1961), p. 2; also see pp. 180–83; also see Robert Presthus' excellent study, *The Organizational Society* (New York, 1962).

[41] (Detroit, 1962).

[42] *Ibid.*, p. 119.

literal tyranny of the majority, but rather the rise of a demagogue nurtured by the destructive forces of "the law of quantities." [43]

The key to the survival of democracy, in Sartori's eyes, rests in the hands of the ruling elite, an elite whose power is based upon recognized superiority. Since a ruling elite exists in all societies, including democratic ones, he holds that it is ridiculous to purge the concept of its traditional connotation regarding the superiority of the few.[44] Unfortunately, Sartori does not indicate what he means by superiority. Would he say, for instance, that the British electorate chose poorly in favoring Atlee over Churchill in 1945, or that American voters overlooked a man of talent such as Stevenson in selecting Eisenhower in 1952? On many counts it could be argued that in both cases the voters bypassed the superior for the inferior man. Democratically viewed, however, it could be contended that the victorious candidates in both countries were superior in the important respect that they more closely reflected the temper and aspirations of the people.

It is doubtful whether Sartori would be persuaded by an argument along these lines since, among other reasons, he sees the chief function of the elite as holding the masses back, to restrain them from the temptations of what he calls perfectionism and the pitfalls of demagoguery. As Sartori put it: "Democracy is terribly difficult. It is so difficult that only expert and accountable elites can save it from the excesses of perfectionism, from the vortex of demagogy, and from the degeneration of the *lex majoris partis*. And this is why adequate leadership is vital to democracy. . . . When the pressure from below is greatest that eminent leadership is more necessary than ever. For it is at this point that perfectionism on the one hand, and mass manipulation and mobilization on the other, throw the system off balance." [45]

The Herculean task which Sartori expects from democratic leadership is hardly credible. If the masses endanger the system either because they are degenerate or because they demand "perfectionism," what *democratic* resources can leaders utilize to avert catastrophe? Moreover, how is the leadership expected to gen-

[43] *Ibid.,* p. 102.
[44] *Ibid.,* p. 112.
[45] *Ibid.,* p. 119.

erate sufficient power *democratically* to exploit the resources that
are required to do the job? Sartori has no answer to these questions.[46]

In emphasizing the role of elites as the core of democratic
theory, Sartori consistently and boldly argues that the purpose
of elections is not to enhance democracy but to select leadership
of the best quality. Since he has little confidence in the judgment
of the people, he hardly could, as indeed he did not, expect them
to exercise that degree of discrimination necessary to choose competent
leaders. As he concisely put it, at the present time the
quantitative instrument of elections "has quickly usurped the
place of the qualitative." [47] For Sartori the corrective does not

[46] Bertrand de Jouvenel, who subscribes to a similar although more moderate
position than Sartori's, does address himself to this problem. He argues
that while "initiatives should be allowed, encouraged, fostered" throughout
society, the government must be responsible for "the preservation of security
in the course of change." The government is thus often required to
disregard the wishes of the people to protect the "imperative of equilibrium."
The primary function of government, de Jouvenel argues, is "to
solve the problems posed by the social actions of free men, and this essential
task may be incompatible with deference to the demands of citizens for
a given action by itself." *Sovereignty* (Chicago, 1957), p. 303.

Similar to Sartori, the government stands guard against the "excesses of
perfectionism," to use Sartori's term, but unlike the Italian political scientists,
de Jouvenel realizes that the government can only effectively perform its
task if it is supported by the "public spirit." In de Jouvenel's words: "The
foregoing remarks should not, then, be mistaken for a plea of greater political
independence for those in office. What they stress is that the performance
of the function of sovereignty depends upon the public spirit."

Despite de Jouvenel's disclaimer, government officials would have considerably
greater independence than under the customary constitutional
systems, since they would judge a proposal not only on the basis of its
merits but also on the basis of its possible disruptive effects in the future.
If it misjudged the "public spirit," its stand could possibly be overridden by
the force of public outcry, but at least initially it would exercise this
prerogative of independence.

What he proposes, in effect, is the adoption of a United States Supreme
Court to veto all measures which are likely, in the view of the membership
of the Court, to disrupt public order. Ironically, the United States Supreme
Court has created more public disturbance by its decisions in recent years
than practically any other political force in the country.

[47] Sartori, p. 104.

rest in educating the electorate in an attempt to inculcate higher standards conducive to the selection of better qualified leaders. The only recourse for democracies is to soften the impact of majority selection through "constitutional techniques," such as by adopting the system of proportional representation.[48] In addition to its superiority in producing better leadership, Sartori argues that proportional representation is also a superior system since — unlike the English two-party system — it invariably produces coalition governments which make it more difficult for the electorate "to pin down who is responsible. . . ."[49]

In sum, the main thrust of his book is unmistakably clear: democracy's worst enemy is itself, and its survival depends upon a retreat from its excesses.[50] The emphasis must now be placed upon the fundamental facts that "democracy is a variant — the open variant — of the elite principle"[51] and that it "has the virtue of bringing out the vital role of leadership, as it implies that minorities are a *sine qua non* condition of the system."[52] Again, Sartori is silent on how the elites, singlehandedly, are to carry the day when they are saddled with incompetent, demanding, and untrustworthy masses.

V

Social pluralism — characterized by a wide diffusion of and competitiveness between elites — has customarily been regarded as the fundamental barrier to the aggrandizement of the state and to

[48] *Ibid.*, p. 109.

[49] *Ibid.*, p. 107.

[50] In warning against excessive democratic idealism, Sartori writes: "So long as democracy remains an ideal that opposes autocracy we can maximize it beyond measure. In fact, the more we exaggerate it the more efficacious it may be. But this is no longer the case once democracy takes the place of its defeated adversary. At this point the deontology (ethical norm) no longer has the task of destroying an inimical system but has, instead, the task of enhancing the system it has created. If, therefore, the *ought* remains unchanged, it begins operating in reverse . . . (The more a democracy is actually maximized, the more the democratic deontology must be minimized.)" (p. 65).

[51] This is true, he argues, since it "allows a free and diffuse circulation of elites . . ." (p. 85).

[52] *Ibid.*, p. 126.

the arbitrary exercise of power by nongovernmental elites. But in his sociological analysis of mass society, William Kornhauser views social pluralism primarily as a fundamental barrier to the rise of the masses.[53] This shift in emphasis of the role of pluralism in a free society is, I believe, significant in the development of the theory of democratic elitism.

In conceiving of pluralism as a two-way shield, a shield which restrains elite power, to be sure, but one which acts chiefly as a protection against mass revolt, Kornhauser approaches, in a challenging and sophisticated manner, the problem of stabilizing what he chooses to call the pluralist society. The threat to pluralism is, of course, mass society, which he defines as "a social system in which elites are readily accessible to influence by non-elites and non-elites are readily available for mobilization by elites."[54] He stresses the point that neither a high accessibility of elites nor a high availability of non-elites is, independent of the other, a sufficient condition to produce the mass society. Both factors must be operative at the same time. Non-elite access to elites is a condition, but not a sufficient one, since non-elites, owing to the impact of societal values and the structure of pluralism, may be self-restrained from exerting excessive and direct influence on elites.[55] For the same reason, the availability of non-elites is also not a sufficient condition since elites, owing to their values, such as attachment to constitutionalism and to the democratic rules of the game, may be restrained from exploiting the opportunity to mobilize the masses.[56]

According to Kornhauser, in other words, the threat of mass society comes from both sides, the masses and the elites. However, it is not elites *qua* elites that threaten the system, but counter-elites, as distinguished from existing or old elites.[57] In sharp contrast to counter-elites, who rise from the mass and who are unrestrained and unattached to prevailing values, established elites have a stake in the going concern and are restrained both by

[53] *The Politics of Mass Society* (Free Press, 1959).
[54] *Ibid.*, p. 39.
[55] *Ibid.*, pp. 29–30.
[56] *Ibid.*, pp. 34–35.
[57] *Ibid.*, p. 33.

their own value commitments to the system and by the conflicting power of other established elites.[58] Thus these elites are not
regarded by Kornhauser as a danger to the system; in fact they
are its protectors. It is they who, owing to their values and abilities, must protect the institutions and standards of the society.[59]
But to perform the task adequately they require a considerable
degree of independence and freedom from interference, especially direct interference, from non-elites. "Direct access to
elites," Kornhauser tells us, "creates a type of elite that lacks adequate inner resources as well as sufficient protection from external
pressures to act with decisiveness and independence. People in a
mass (that is, available non-elites) are inclined to adopt populist
values, including diffuse anti-elitist and strongly egalitarian sentiments." [60]

Thus, as envisaged by Kornhauser, a pluralistic social structure
performs a dual function; first, in keeping people absorbed in
proximate concerns of everyday life — in their work, family,
church, and the like — it minimizes their availability for mobilization by counter-elites; [61] and, secondly, in performing this task, it
greatly mitigates mass pressure and demands that would otherwise
hobble the independence of elites essential to their maintaining the system. However, to protect society fully, a strong intermediate group structure is also required. Non-elites can hardly be
expected to be completely absorbed by nonpolitical activities on
the proximate level; hence when they do voice their political
demands, these must be "filtered through intervening relationships." [62] In stressing the importance of this point, Kornhauser
writes: "Elites are more directly influenced by non-elites in the
absence of intermediate groups because they are *less insulated*.
Elites lose their insulation since demands and impulses of large
numbers of people that formerly were *sublimated and fulfilled*
by intermediate groups now are focused directly on the national
level. Higher elites absorb functions formerly reserved to inter-

[58] *Ibid.*, pp. 36–37.
[59] *Ibid.*, p. 52.
[60] *Ibid.*, pp. 59–60.
[61] *Ibid.*, p. 64.
[62] *Ibid.*, p. 76.

mediate elites and therefore no longer can depend on these groups to *siphon off popular pressures* and to regulate participation. Furthermore, popular participation in the higher elites is all the stronger and less restrained for being in part a *substitute for diversified participation* in intermediate groups – especially in times of crisis." [63]

In sum, Kornhauser expects the pluralist structure, when it is operating effectively, to act as a buffer – on both the proximate and intermediate levels – between masses and elites. In insulating each from the other, it protects the democratic system from the vulnerability of mass politics by allowing the established elites, unencumbered by the masses, to fulfill their role as guardians of the system. It is a democratic system, in Kornhauser's view, since political leaders are restrained by competition among themselves and are accountable to the people at periodic elections. He is quick to add, however, that between elections the system should afford "considerable autonomy for those who win positions of leadership." [64]

Unlike Sartori, who relies upon the political elites to hold the masses somehow at bay, Kornhauser shows that a viable social pluralism will *automatically* and *effectively* do the job without relying upon either the good graces of the masses or the conscious efforts of the elites! Thus his appeal is directed at fortifying and strengthening social pluralism.

But how viable must a pluralist system be to be immune to a demagogic takeover? In light of McCarthyism, American pluralism apparently has not reached a sufficiently high degree of viability. In the absence of a vigorous attack on the root problem of social alienation, does not the American system remain vulnerable to attack? This question, within the context of Kornhauser's analysis, confronts us with a basic dilemma: if reform is required to eradicate alienation, will it not stir up mass agitation, releasing the masses from their insulated positions, leading to demands founded upon "populist values, including diffuse anti-elitist and strongly egalitarian sentiments"? Put differently, how can essential reforms in a democracy be instituted without the support of

[63] *Ibid.*, p. 99. Italics are mine.
[64] *Ibid.*, p. 230.

the masses, yet if their support is solicited, will not the movement be in danger of subversion by "mass values"? On the other hand, if the risk of reform is considered too great, will not the system remain exposed to a recurrence of demagoguery?

Founded as they are upon the premise that the people are not to be trusted, the theories of Sartori and Kornhauser do not effectively come to grips with this dilemma. There is, however, an alternative approach to this problem — also within the bounds of democratic elitism — which will receive our attention in the next chapter.

4
Elite
consensus

A WIDESPREAD public commitment to the fundamental norms underlying the democratic process was regarded
by classical democratic theorists as essential to the survival of
democracy.[1] For without a strong commitment to freedom, the
people would be likely to make extreme and anti-democratic demands upon government; moreover, in the absence of such a commitment, the people could not be relied upon to stand vigilant
against the encroachment of freedom by political elites. Today
social scientists, as we have seen, tend to reject this position. They
do so not only because of their limited confidence in the commitment of non-elites to freedom, but also because of the growing
awareness that non-elites are, in large part, politically activated
by elites. The empirical finding that mass behavior is generally in
response to the attitudes, proposals, and modes of action of political elites [2] gives added support to the position that the respon-

[1] For a critical analysis of the doctrine "agreement on fundamentals,"
see Carl J. Friedrich, *Man and His Government* (New York, 1963), pp.
237–38 and pp. 345–46.
[2] See V. O. Key, Jr., *Public Opinion and American Democracy* (New
York, 1961); and Fred I. Greenstein, *The American Party System and the
American People* (Englewood Cliffs, N.J., 1963), pp. 5–36, and the biblio-
graphy cited.

sibility for maintaining "the rules of the game" rests not on the shoulders of the people but on those of the elites. In concluding his study, *Public Opinion and Democracy*, the late V.O. Key, Jr., wrote:

> The masses do not corrupt themselves; if they are corrupted, they have been corrupted. . . . The critical element for the health of a democratic order consists in the beliefs, standards, and competence of those who constitute the influentials, the opinion-leaders, the political activists in the order. That group, as has been made plain, refuses to define itself with great clarity in the American system; yet analysis after analysis points to its existence. If a democracy tends toward indecision, decay, and disaster, the responsibility rests here, not in the mass of people.[3]

If, as Key asserted, the responsibility for the survival of democracy rests with elites, not the masses of the people, what precisely is required for an elite to meet its responsibility? Is it sufficient that each elite adhere to the rules of the game in the struggle to further its own interest? Or in addition must it transcend its selfish interests and, in cooperation with other elites, police the system? Must responsible elites, in short, combine "autonomy with co-operation," [4] conflict with consensus? Professor Key more or less sidestepped this problem, but in passing he stated: "Among the upper-activist stratum a consensus does need to prevail on the technical rules of the game by which the system operates." [5] However, a growing number of social scientists have directed their attention to the problem of the necessity and feasibility of elite consensus in a democracy. For example, David Truman argues

[3] Key, *op. cit.*, p. 558.

[4] "A unified elite," writes Raymond Aron, "means the end of freedom. But when the groups of the elite are not only distinct but become a disunity, it means the end of the State. Freedom survives in those intermediate regions, which are continually threatened when there is moral unity of the elite, where men and groups preserve the secret of single and eternal wisdom and have learnt how to combine autonomy with co-operation." "Social Structure and the Ruling Class," *British Journal of Sociology* (vol. I, no. 2, June, 1950), p. 129. For a similar view, see Suzanne Keller, *Beyond the Ruling Class* (New York, 1963), pp. 74, 146, and 220; and J. P. Nehl, "Consensus or Elite Domination: The Case of Business," *Political Studies* (Fall, 1965), pp. 22–44.

[5] Key, *op. cit.*, p. 555.

that the continuing existence of the democratic process depends on the "consensus of elites," as a necessary basis upon which established elites can repulse the attempts of demagogues to subvert the system.[6] In his discussion of the corporation, A. A. Berle, Jr., contends that corporate power must, in the last analysis, be held accountable to elite groups.[7] Despite his vigorous attack on the "power elite," the late C. Wright Mills did not advocate that it should be radically disturbed. Instead he argued that the "power elite" must be made responsible to the humanizing force of an intellectual elite.[8]

These three men are in different areas of social science, and in some major respects their positions are fundamentally in conflict, but, at the same time, their theories concerning the relation of elites and democracy are strikingly similar. The three are deeply concerned with the present state of American democratic society, agreeing that substantial change is required as a means to preserve or strengthen it. Further, not one of the three advocates dismantling the power elites which each, in a different way, believes to exist. Truman relies upon the "intervening structure of elites" to save the democratic system. Mills viewed the existing structure of the "power elite" as an opportunity unique in history for man to determine his own fate. Berle's high regard for the productive machine of capitalism leads to his favorable disposition toward the power of the relatively few men who are instrumental in its direction. Moreover, the creation of a new or a more self-conscious elite group is central to the argument of each theorist. The discussion in this chapter of the theories of these men will perhaps throw light on a question which is central to democratic elitism: If elite consensus is essential to the health of democratic pluralism, is it compatible with what we have been led to understand is a basic feature and requirement of the system — effective and regularized restraint of elite power resulting from the division and competitiveness among elites?

[6] "The American System in Crisis," *Political Science Quarterly* (December, 1959), pp. 481–97.

[7] *Power Without Property* (New York, 1959), and his discussion in W. H. Ferry, *Economy Under Law* (Santa Barbara, Cal., 1960), pp. 51–68.

[8] *Causes of World War Three* (New York, 1958), pp. 36–42 and 131–37.

I

Central to Truman's thesis is the assumption that power within the system resides primarily with the "intervening structure of elites" — with those persons who hold leading positions in the giant corporations, trade unions, churches, political parties, and professional and veteran organizations. In contrast to the elites, the masses of ordinary people are powerless since they "cannot act except through organization and in response to the initiative of small numbers of leaders." [9] The stability of the system, indeed its very survival, depends upon the elites. This is not a weakness of the system; to the contrary, in Truman's eyes, it is its strength. He reasons: "Being more influential, they [the elites] are privileged; and, being privileged, they have, with few exceptions, a special stake in the continuation of the political system on which their privileges rest." [10] In his view, nevertheless, the system is vulnerable to extinction since it will have difficulty withstanding major recurring challenges from abroad, challenges of the magnitude of the Chinese debacle of the 1940's and of the Sputnik crisis in 1957. Evoking frustration, a sense of failure, and fear of a general incomprehensibility of the situation, such challenges can lead to a frantic irrational response from the American public.

The specter of Senator McCarthy is very much before Truman's eyes. He believes that a similar threat is almost bound to arise again, and unless the nongovernmental elites acquire sufficient maturity to be aware of the nature of the threat and the need to act against it quickly and decisively, the system as we know it will be destroyed. Although Truman believes that the elites are capable of reaching such maturity, he is pessimistically inclined as to whether they actually will.[11]

[9] Truman, *op. cit.*, p. 489.

[10] *Ibid.*, p. 489.

[11] Truman's position is somewhat similar to Karl Mannheim's concern for the fate of democracy expressed over twenty years ago. He believed that the proliferation of elites in a democracy tends to decrease the influence of any one elite, for they cancel each other out. Thus the society becomes leaderless, creating power vacuums which demagogues can easily

What is startling about Truman's thesis is that with one sweep of the pen he has practically relegated to obsolescence his magnum opus, *The Governmental Process*.[12] The major point of his earlier book is that the governmental process is stable; that it tends toward the maintenance of an equilibrium; and that interest groups and their leaders are kept within bounds by the restraint of overlapping membership and the activation of potential groups if constitutional norms are violated. The emphasis, in other words, is placed on the role of the rank and file member and the unorganized. Potential groups, representing majority interests, Truman had contended, "are significant not only because they may become the basis for organized interest groups but because the membership of such potential groups overlap extensively the memberships of various organized interest groups. . . . It is this multiple membership in potential groups based on widely held and accepted interests that serve as a balance wheel in a going political system like that of the United States." [13]

---

exploit in their rise to power. "They meet with no real resistance," Mannheim wrote, "because all the elites from whom values, taste, and standards of judgment could emanate, have cancelled each other out. The established elites under threat become acutely sensitive to new experience, but the chances of an enduring pattern of response emerging are very slight." *Man and Society in an Age of Reconstruction* (London, 1946), pp. 87–88.

Unlike Truman, however, Mannheim believed that more was required of the established elites than to stand guard against the threat of the demagogue. What was required was conscious planning which attacked "the sources of maladjustment in the social order on the basis of a thorough knowledge of the whole mechanism of society and the way in which it works." *Ibid.*, p. 114.

The British political scientist J. P. Nehl believes, as does Truman, that an elite consensus is essential for all sophisticated societies. "I believe that to have a consensus *at all*, you need an ideal type, a model of attitudes, procedures, institutions — an elite. This must not be socially so remote as to make emulation and effective entry impossible. You also need a vehicle that will effectively carry the consensus into society. In Britain this is the higher Civil Service" (p. 29). His whole theory of consensus is built on the belief that "elite Consensus is not so much the product of compromise as of elite ascendancy and its acceptance." *Op. cit.*, p. 41.

[12] (New York, 1951.)

[13] *Ibid.*, pp. 512 and 514.

But in his more recent "American System in Crisis," [14] he says, in effect, that the primary characteristic of the political system is not its stability but its instability; that the chief threat to the system does not stem from the activities of self-seeking leaders of established organizations in the struggle for power, but from the demagogue, rising suddenly out of political chaos; and finally, that the main safeguard against the infraction of constitutional procedures no longer resides in the non-elite mechanism of overlapping membership and potential groups, but rests exclusively with persons who are currently in positions of privilege and power. What heretofore was considered the potential threat to the system is now regarded as its guardian.

Assuming the soundness of Truman's reappraisal of the political scene, what is the likelihood that the established elites will be able to reach a consensus from which they will be in a position to intervene on behalf of the system? To what extent, in other words, is "consensus of elites" within the context of Truman's analysis a realistic concept? Truman recognizes some of the difficulties involved: that the views of some elites are too narrow for them to be aware of the system as a whole, while others are too preoccupied with their own substantive struggle to be truly concerned with the general well-being of the political process; and that even if elites do perceive a threat to the system, it is difficult, because of the looseness of the elite structure, for them to reach a general consensus as to what action is appropriate. However, despite these practical difficulties, he believes that in principle "consensus of elites" is a fundamentally sound concept. For, he argues, it is based on the rock of self-interest, self-interest of the privileged and the influential "in the continuation of the political system on which their privileges rest." [15]

His argument is based on the tacit assumption that reasonable men agree on what constitute the fundamental procedures of democracy. In the abstract the assumption is tenable, but it is considerably less so when procedure is entangled in substantive issues which are deeply controversial. The McCarthy issue, for example, reflected the close connection between substantive

[14] See note 6.
[15] *Ibid.*, p. 489.

and procedural issues. Consensus on the meaning and scope of freedom of speech, to cite another example, is inevitably transformed into sharp disagreement when this right is exercised by the Communist, the bigot, the bookseller of obscene material, the picket, or the employer speaking to a captive labor audience. There is general agreement that Congress' power of investigation is not unlimited, that it must not violate the canons of fair procedure. But what constitutes these canons has been highly contested when placed within a political context. When Congress shifted its focus of investigation from business in the 1930's to subversive activities in the postwar period, it was not surprising to find that liberals and conservatives changed sides on this issue. So it is with most procedural rules; they cannot be extricated from the substantive interests and values with which they interact without being disembodied of their essential meaning.

If, then, procedural norms cannot realistically be dissociated from the political context in which they operate and the substantive values and interests which they affect, the requirements for reaching a consensus on fundamental procedure are considerably greater than Truman has suggested. It is not a question of elites transcending their vested interests to reach a consensus on procedural norms, but rather to reach a consensus on the substantive issues underlying the procedural norms under attack. This they clearly failed to do during Senator McCarthy's bid for power prior to his confrontation of President Eisenhower and the Army. It was not that elites were unaware that he was violating traditional norms of due process and freedom of speech. Their inability to reach consensus was more likely due to a profound disagreement as to what constituted the major threat to internal security — Communism and/or social reform, or the investigations against un-American activities — as well as to differing appraisals as to the vulnerability of the system to subversion. As long as the Senator confined his attack to New Dealers and suspected Communists, some elites could afford the ambivalent attitude of "I do not approve of his method, but . . ." In retrospect it appears that the substantive basis for an elite consensus in defense of procedural norms did not exist until McCarthy challenged, in addition to his old foes, the power of the Republican Administration and the Army.[16]

Truman's concept of "consensus of elites" is open to another and, in my judgment, a more important criticism. If his plea for more aware, self-conscious elites capable of forming a "broad, conceptual perception of the threats to the system" [17] were realized, what would keep the self-conscious elites within constitutional bounds? If the self-appointed guardians are capable of protecting the system, is there not a danger that under some circumstances they would be capable of subverting it? To discount this danger on the ground that established elites identify their interest with the constitutional norms of the system is as sound as reliance upon natural law as an effective restraint against an arbitrary rule.[18] The major weakness in both positions is that neither the privilege of elites nor their view of natural law is under all conditions necessarily in harmony with constitutionalism. For example, a democratic and broadly based attack on privilege could very likely be interpreted by powerful elites as an attack on the system. In such a case they could hardly be expected to disassociate their privileged position from the political foundations upon which their privilege rests. To contend, therefore, that elites must become the guardians of the system is either to freeze democracy within narrow bounds — bounds within which established elites are not threatened — or to endanger the existence of democracy. For, under Truman's theory, the democratic process is secure as long as established elites are able to combat any major challenge to their privilege; it becomes insecure, however, to the extent that a reform movement success-

[16] In attacking Talcott Parsons' proposal that business leaders should join political and cultural elites in a "closed alliance" to protect civil liberties, Andrew Hacker writes, "For all the rhetoric about 'the conscience of the corporation' and 'the social responsibilities of business,' when the chips are down the elite has shown itself unwilling to oppose the pathological strains which Parsons deplores." "Sociology and Ideology" in M. Black (ed.), *The Social Theories of Talcott Parsons* (Englewood Cliffs, N.J.), p. 307.

[17] *Op. cit.*, p. 497.

[18] For a neo-natural law position, see Walter Lippmann, *Essays in the Public Philosophy* (Boston, 1955).

fully meets the challenge of elites and thereby weakens the essential supports of the system. As elite power diminishes, in other words, guardians would not be in a position to keep the system within traditional bounds. Furthermore, their allegiance to the system would lessen as the gap between it and their privilege widens.

Truman's basic assumption [19] — that privilege and democracy are not only compatible but mutually interdependent — is simply not borne out by analysis. He has clearly detected a fundamental deficiency of the American democratic system. But it cannot be alleviated by an appeal to elites; for them to become "self-conscious of power and responsibility" would deepen, not lessen, the crisis of American democracy.

II

C. Wright Mills's *Power Elite* [20] is more than an attempted documentation of the thesis that an elite actually exists which determines basic policy for the nation. For this seemingly empirical treatise is capped by the judgment that the power elite is irresponsible, immoral, and ignorant.[21] The inference of the book is unmistakable; the existing elite structure should be dismantled. This inference is re-enforced by Mills's argument in the *Causes of World War Three* [22] that "any serious fight for peace" necessitates an attack especially on the ascendancy of the military and the corporate elite.[23]

But what is particularly interesting about Mills's thought is that, in reality, he did not want the existing elite structure to be disturbed. He rejected such a course out of practicality, among other reasons. "There is neither," Mills wrote, "constitutional nor revolutionary opposition to the existing structure of power or the type of men who run it. So neither 'practical' nor 'revolutionary' programs just now can very well form the serious content of all

---

[19] This assumption was also basic to William Kornhauser's theory. The criticism here also applies consequently to Kornhauser. See Chapter 3.

[20] (New York, 1956.)

[21] *Ibid.*, pp. 350, 361.

[22] (New York, 1958.)

[23] *Ibid.* (paperback edition), pp. 120–21.

our criticisms, programs, demands." [24] This position is re-enforced by his pessimistic appraisal of the political health of the electorate. In contrast with an increasingly unified and co-ordinate power elite, he held that the great majority of people are politically fragmented, passive, and powerless.[25] Throughout his writings he was insistent that genuine publics, in John Dewey's meaning of the term, are rapidly becoming extinct in America. Consequently, ordinary men are unable to translate their personal troubles into social issues and discuss them in terms of the general well-being of the community and the nation.[26] Whether Mills would have reached this finding if it were not essential to his central thesis — that the power elite is unencumbered by the bottom and middle strata of society — is conjectural. Nonetheless, having made the point, he cannot very well turn around and make a case for radical reform based upon the political power of the people. But there is a more basic reason than impracticality to explain Mills's aversion to seriously proposing an attack on the power elite.

In the tradition of all sciences, Mills was a rationalist, believing that the extent of man's freedom is dependent, above all, on his ability to reason and to perceive reality. Accordingly, he argued that within the context of social science, the challenge is to understand the existing social structure and its interacting forces "in an attempt to find points of effective intervention, in order to know what can and what must be structurally changed if the role of explicit decision in history-making is to be enlarged." [27] That is, if we are to be free in the sense of directing our own fate, an enlarged and centralized means of decision-making is essential. For knowledge, Mills argued, is of little avail in determining the course of events if power is widely diffused. However, "in those societies in which the means of power are enormous in scope and centralized in form a few men may be so placed within the historical structure that by their decisions

[24] *Ibid.*, p. 134.
[25] *Power Elite, op. cit.*, Chapter 13.
[26] *Sociological Imagination* (New York, 1959), pp. 188–91; also *Power Elite*, Chapter 13.
[27] *Sociological Imagination, op. cit.*, p. 174.

about the use of these means they modify the structural conditions under which most men live." [28] For this reason Mills could view the trend toward the centralization of power optimistically. "The rise of the power elite," he wrote, "is a token of the centralization of the means of history-making itself — and this fact opens up new opportunities for the willful making of history." [29]

Thus the fundamental problem for Mills is how the gap between power and knowledge can be closed. Today the intellectual is dominated and his talents exploited by the willful men of power. The relationship, Mills argued, must be reversed: decisions of power must be made responsible to the "free intellect." [30] Only then will man be in a position to determine his own fate.

Clearly, then, to attack the structure of power or the power elite itself is to jeopardize this goal. For a successful democratic assault on the citadel of power could easily bring about the destruction of the existing centralized structure of decision-making. Such a probability must have been apparent to Mills since his own definition of democracy implies a decentralized system of decision-making: "democracy implies that those vitally affected by any decision men make have an effective voice in that decision." [31] Even under the assumption that a centralized system of decision-making could be reconciled with his concept of democracy, it is difficult to see how Everyman could have an "effective voice" in a decision which affects him without the final and centralized decision being marked by intellectual impurities. It is quite evident that Mills was deeply ambivalent concerning this problem. He was committed to democracy, continually upbraiding Americans for not "taking democracy seriously," yet this sentiment appeared to be overbalanced by his belief that in the modern world history-making could be rationally determined. Thus, despite his democratic aversion to "men of power," he could not bring himself to advocate the abolition of the power elite here and now.

For Mills the political problem was not to destroy the structure

[28] *Causes of World War Three, op. cit.,* p. 13.
[29] *Ibid.,* p. 37.
[30] *Sociological Imagination, op. cit.,* p. 183; *Causes,* Chapter 7.
[31] *Sociological Imagination,* p. 188.

of power, but rather to make the decisions of the powerful responsible. But on the key question — responsible to whom? — Mills equivocated. In an attempt to reconcile power, knowledge, and democracy, he wrote:

> Those who decide should be held responsible to those men and women everywhere who are in any grievous way affected by decisions and defaults. But by whom should they be held responsible? That is the immediate problem of political power. In both East and West today, the immediate answer is: By the intellectual community. Who else but intellectuals are capable of discerning the role in history of explicit history-making decisions? Who else is in a position to understand that now fate itself must be made a political issue? [32]

In effect, the power elite in Mills's theory must be held accountable to the intellectual elite. Ideally, decision-makers should be held responsible to the people, but since ordinary men lack the knowledge to direct "history-making decisions," the responsibility falls upon intellectuals. The democratic principle of the will of the majority apparently is only operative when majority will and truth are interchangeable. In somewhat the same vein as the theory of the dictatorship of the proletariat, Mills's men of knowledge must direct society's destiny until conditions exist when ordinary men are able to discern the truth.

If man's fate depends upon closing the power-knowledge gap, how is this to be done? How can pivotal decisions by men of power be influenced by and answerable to men of knowledge? The task for intellectuals, Mills held, is to free themselves from their present bondage as "technicians, hired publicists and intellectual dupes" of the power elite.[33] More important, in becoming "free intellects," they must become "an independent and oppositional group," grounded on the consensus that the cold war policies of the two major powers are fundamentally wrong.[34]

Mills had no illusions that a direct appeal by intellectuals to those in power would have any visible effect, but he did believe that indirectly, through public pressures, the intellectual elite would be able to assert its influence upon decision-makers. In

[32] *Causes*, p. 26.
[33] *Ibid.*, pp. 134, 144; *Sociological Imagination*, p. 193.
[34] *Causes*, p. 144.

sharp contrast to the *Power Elite*, in which the mass nature of society is underscored, we now find in the *Causes* that at least some publics exist and are sufficiently vital so that public debate and exposure will be consequential and meaningful in the shaping of national policy.

Even assuming the validity of his major thesis, Mills's position on the role of the intellectual is inadequate on two counts. First, if intellectuals have been "bought off," as he argued, then it seems utopian to assume that they could be persuaded to transcend their material interest and the prevailing ideology of their country. Second, even if intellectuals did become "free," there is little reason to assume that they would be able to reach a consensus on basic values underlying the issues of the cold war. While Mills did envisage disagreement and debate among intellectuals on some issues, he found it inconceivable for genuine intellectuals to disagree on major issues concerning the cold war. "This disgraceful cold war," he wrote, "is surely a war in which we as intellectuals ought at once to become conscientious objectors." He came close to defining an intellectual as one who opposes such policies; all others are "intellectual dupes of political patrioteers." [35]

Mills had great confidence in the ability of social science to overcome the social and political ills of man. But in his enthusiasm to see knowledge triumph over power, he unwittingly assumed that his position on resolving the major issues of the cold war was true. Trapped by this error, he believed that intellectuals, once free, could easily reach consensus on the basic issues of war and peace. In fact, he believed this consensus could span the globe, unifying intellectuals everywhere, including Soviet intellectuals. In Mills's words, "As intellectuals of the world we should awake and unite with intellectuals everywhere." [36]

III

A. A. Berle has developed a theory of "public consensus" in an effort to legitimize the growing concentration of corporate power. In his recent re-examination of the corporate structure in America,

[35] *Ibid.*, p. 144.
[36] *Ibid.*, p. 145.

he observes that "the thrust of economic influence on life is increasingly administered by a relatively small group of individuals," who as corporation managers are essentially civil servants "seeking reputation, power and a pension. . . ." [37] These self-perpetuating men of corporate power can claim legitimacy through the undying myth that management is held responsible by stockholder elections. But this fiction is no longer necessary to sustain managerial power, since its legitimacy, Berle argues, can be defended on the solid ground of "public consensus." He is intent upon a defense of this elite, since, in his view, it has developed a "superb productive machine." [38] For this reason he believes that "economic power perhaps is best located in a sort of government of best minds," namely, in the minds of the managerial elite. [39] Thus, like Truman and Mills, he does not want to divest the established elite of its power.

The solution of the problem of power as far as the managerial elites are concerned, Berle holds, is not to "change the corporate structure but to change managers when they abuse their power." [40] And this can and is being done through the force of "the public consensus." He conceives of "the public consensus" as general and unstated premises concerning public morality, amorphous in nature but nonetheless real. Managers, he is convinced, are quite aware of its reality and respect its power when activated in the form of public opinion. [41] The "public consensus" therefore acts as both a restraint and as a remedy to wrong-doing. The key question is, of course, who activates the transformation of the public consensus into the politically potent public opinion? Similar to Mills, Berle places the responsibility on the intellectual elite: the university professors, the specialists, the responsible

[37] *Power Without Property, op. cit.,* pp. 117–18.

[38] Ferry, *The Economy Under Law, op. cit.,* p. 53.

[39] *Power Without Property,* p. 109. He believes that eventually the fiduciary institutions will take over power. "Ultimately," he says, "a relatively small oligarchy of men operating in the same atmosphere, absorbing the same information, moving in the same circles and in a relatively small world knowing each other, dealing with each other, and having more in common than differences, will hold the reins." *Ibid.,* p. 53.

[40] *Ibid.,* p. 87.

[41] *Ibid.,* pp. 110–15.

journalists, and the respected politicians. "These, and men like them," Berle states, "are thus the real tribunal to which the American system is finally accountable."[42]

It is probably true that "public consensus" acts as a restraint against anti-social action by management. But business scandals, periodically uncovered by federal law enforcement agencies and legislative investigations (rather than by intellectuals), suggest the imperfection of Berle's safeguard. Intellectuals can hardly be expected to live up to Berle's expectations when corporate behavior by small and influential groups is shrouded in secrecy and when pertinent information released to the public is first "processed" by public relations experts. Moreover, owing to the widespread instances of wrong-doing throughout American life, it is doubtful whether the fiber of "public consensus" has not been materially softened by a sizeable dose of cynicism. For example, it was an open question for top management of the electric equipment companies whether executives who were convicted of crimes should be released from their positions. It is further significant that "public consensus" did not come close to jeopardizing the posts of top management in those firms, despite the strongly worded dictum of the court that they had undoubtedly been aware of and morally responsible for the fraud.[43]

These objections aside, Berle's concept of the "public consensus," at best, restrains corporate power only on marginal issues. It is confined to the procedural rules of the game, leaving unencumbered the decision-making power of management on crucial substantive issues that materially affect the community and the nation. To justify such power in the hands of the few on the ground that they have built a "superb productive machine" is to overlook the question: the machine, for whom and for what?

In less than two years after making his case for the legitimatizing of managerial power under the guidance of "public consensus," Berle did come to grips with the larger question. In a discussion with his colleagues at the Center for the Study of Democratic Institutions, he implicitly concedes that something more is required than a "public consensus" to enforce the rules of the

[42] *Ibid.*, p. 113.
[43] John Grant Fuller, *Gentlemen Conspirators* (New York, 1962).

game and the profit motive to give direction to the economy.[44] This something more Berle dubs the "transcendental margin." He conceives of it as "something extra-economic in motivation, some philosophical ideal of what a good life is and what a good community is." [45] For the decision-making power of the managerial elite to be legitimate, then, it must conform on the negative side to the "public consensus," and respond on the positive side to the directive of the "transcendental margin."

For Berle the existence of the "transcendental margin" depends upon the consensus of individuals, individuals who have the capacity to think philosophically. Because of the inability of a great number of people to think philosophically, "this is really where," Berle says, "you have to have what you call an elite, although I hate the word." [46] He again looks to the university as the haven for the elite, who, as a result of a free exchange of ideas, ought to be able to reach a consensus on what constitutes the "transcendental margin." [47] Like Mills, Berle tacitly assumes that there is somehow a unique and not too difficult basis upon which intellectuals can reach a consensus. I tend to think that the opposite is true: that the capacity to think philosophically lends itself to discerning fine distinctions in substance and approach, and thus opens an inexhaustible source for disagreement and argument. The intellectual process at its best breeds controversy, not agreement. That is why the process contributes most as a catalyst in a democratic society rather than as a dispenser of truth.

IV

It is quite significant, I believe, that none of the theorists discussed in this chapter has been content to rely on either the constitutional system or competitive interaction of elites to solve the problem of power in a democracy. Instead they have turned to some form of "elite consensus" as a means to curb or direct elite power effectively. If the above analysis has been substantially

[44] *Economy Under Law*, pp. 51–58.
[45] *Ibid.*, p. 53.
[46] *Ibid.*, p. 57.
[47] *Ibid.*, pp. 53–58.

sound, the conclusion is inescapable that this concept is basically unrealistic. But what is of greater importance is that the instruments of restraint which heretofore have been central in theories of democratic elitism have been pushed aside. Is this a forewarning that we must look for new methods of curbing power in a society characterized by highly developed elite structures? Are we coming to the stage where our only recourse is to rely on the good graces of those who wield a great amount of power, influence, and authority not to abuse it? This is the inference to be drawn from the theories reviewed here. It is also the inference of the thesis of a social scientist whose recent book, *Beyond the Ruling Class*,[48] focuses on the problem of the role of "strategic elites" and their exercise of power in a democracy.

Throughout her book, Suzanne Keller reasserts her conviction: "The proliferation and partial autonomy of strategic elites, their variation in composition and recruitment, and differing moral perspectives decrease the likelihood of an omnipotent oligarchy. In addition, these elites critically examine — and thereby check each other's actions and decisions. Thus limited power leads to limited abuses." [49] However, despite the autonomy and diversity of elites, Keller believes that "moral consensus" among "strategic elites" is essential if society is to survive.[50] "Those entrusted with social leadership in various spheres," she states, "must be able to act independently and yet strive to present a united moral front." [51] If this objective is to be achieved, elites must have self-assurance for their own social superiority, which, she believes, calls for an articulate set of beliefs and ideals justifying their superiority.[52] An ideology of this nature, Keller realizes, is difficult to develop in a democracy. But much like

[48] Suzanne Keller (New York, 1963.)

[49] *Ibid.*, pp. 273–74.

[50] *Ibid.*, p. 126–27.

[51] *Ibid.*, p. 127.

[52] "Community of experience," she states, "does not lead to a community of interests. The latter demands a self-assurance which helps elites accept their existence, instead of, as seems the case in the United States, denying or camouflaging it. It also calls for a set of articulate beliefs and ideals justifying the social superiority required by elites to perform their functions" (p. 220).

Sartori, she argues that it is time that democratic beliefs adjust to the facts of life and to the danger of an "ideological void left when men seek to deny or dare not accept the facts of their elite status." [53]

The independence and differentiation of elites will effectively keep elite power within bounds, yet their "joint destiny," built upon an ideology of elite superiority, will provide the basis for dynamic leadership, promoting the interests of the nation and humanity.[54] How this fine balance between autonomy, self-interest, and strife on the one hand, and unity based on "moral consensus" on the other, can be effectively maintained over any length of time is not explained. It appears to be more of a hope than an expectation to be realized in the near future. In the end, Keller too falls back on the conscience of the elite to refrain from abusing its privileged position.[55]

[53] *Ibid.*, p. 192.
[54] *Ibid.*, pp. 220–21.
[55] *Ibid.*, p. 279.

5
The concept
of political elite

"POLITICAL SCIENCE, as an empirical discipline," Harold Lasswell states, "is the study of the shaping and sharing of power." [1] In this assertion, which is the leading theme of almost all the rich and diverse outpourings of this talented political scientist, Lasswell makes explicit the unarticulated but central premise of Pareto and Mosca. It is not surprising, therefore, that Lasswell, as his predecessors, focuses on the influential and powerful as the object of study. However, he is quick to point out in his various works that the purpose of his scientific explorations is to contribute toward the "policy sciences of democracy, in which the ultimate goal is the realization of human dignity in theory and fact." [2] In conceiving of society in elite-mass terms, he has nevertheless tended toward an elitist approach to the political process. In a somewhat defensive vein Lasswell remarks that

[1] Joint author with Abraham Kaplan, *Power and Society* (New Haven, 1950), p. xiv.

[2] *Policy Sciences, Recent Developments in Scope and Method*, ed. Lasswell and Daniel Lerner (Stanford, 1951), p. 15. This quotation is from Lasswell's own contribution and is quoted by Bernard Crick, *The American Science of Politics* (London, 1959), p. 192.

to concentrate on elites does not imply an indifference toward the rest of the community. "It is impossible to locate the few without considering the many." [3] His claim is not necessarily true. In locating the few, it is not logically imperative to consider the well-being of the many. And by and large Lasswell did not. Nevertheless, the inference of his concept of political elite for modern democratic theory is of major importance.

Lasswell's concept of elite is somewhat confusing since he has rendered various formulations of it over the years, not bothering to say whether a more recent formulation of the concept is intended to supplement or to replace its predecessors. [4] In his earlier writings, the elite was characterized by its ability to get the most values and by its prowess in manipulating the masses. "The few who get the most of any value," he wrote in 1934, "are the elite; the rest, the rank and file. The elite preserves its ascendancy by manipulating symbols, controlling supplies, and applying violence." [5] In his well-known book, *Politics: Who Gets What, When and How,* written two years later, the importance of the manipulative abilities of the elite is also emphasized: "The fate of an elite is profoundly affected by the ways it manipulates the environment; that is to say, by the use of violence, goods, symbols, and practices." [6] Lasswell's stress on elite manipulation during this period was perhaps due to normative as well as scientific reasons. For the conclusions in his pioneer treatise on *Psychopathology and Politics* [7] are predicated upon elite manipulative powers. He discounted the utility of public discussion in promoting mutual understanding and insight on the grounds that "discussion frequently arouses a psychology of conflict which produces obstructive frictions, and irrelevant values." [8] What is needed, therefore, is not the airing of political problems, but the adoption of preventive politics, politics which place the burden, in

[3] *Politics: Who Gets What, When and How* (New York, 1936), p. 309.
[4] See Crick, *op. cit.*, pp. 179–81, for a discussion of Lasswell's general philosophic shift from his earlier to his present position.
[5] *World Politics and Personal Insecurity* (Chicago, 1934), p. 3.
[6] *Politics, Who Gets What, op. cit.*, p. 310; also see pp. 444 and 307.
[7] (Chicago, 1930.)
[8] *Ibid.*, pp. 196–97.

an elitist's fashion, upon social administrators to quash, by manipulative techniques, issues destined for public consideration which, in their judgment, would be detrimental to the public interest. "The achievement of the ideal of preventive politics," Lasswell argued, "depends less upon changes in social organization than on improving the methods and education of social administrators and social scientists." [9]

In his more recent works, two decades later, Lasswell defines elite in terms of the distribution of power rather than of values gained by the few. "The elite are those with most power in a group; mid-elite, those with less power, the mass, least power." [10] And "power is participation in the making of decisions." [11] He therefore regards the political elite as those who comprise "the power holders of a body politic." [12] Defining the political elite as power holders rather than in the more narrow and conventional manner, as those who participate in decision-making *within* government,[13] affords a realistic inclusion within the political

[9] *Ibid.*, pp. 201, 202.

[10] *Power and Society*, p. 201.

[11] *Ibid.*, p. 75.

[12] *The Comparative Study of Elites*, with Daniel Lerner, *et al.* (Stanford, 1952), p. 13. In a somewhat confusing way, the authors also state that the political elite includes "the social formations from which leaders typically come, and to which accountability is maintained." Within the context of this formulation, "the political elite is the top power *class*" (*ibid.*, my italics). However the linkage of the political elite and class is only applicable in a class-bound society in which leaders are regularly recruited from one class. In *Power and Society* (pp. 225–28), Lasswell points out that this obviously would not be the case in a democracy.

[13] For instance, Pareto tends to equate a political elite with a governing elite; the latter, he states, comprises "individuals who directly or indirectly play some considerable part in government, and a *non*-governing elite, comprising the rest" (*Mind and Society*, #2032). Carl Friedrich criticizes Pareto's distinction because it does not clearly demarcate between the political and nonpolitical elites. For Friedrich, a political elite is equivalent to a governing elite, although elites are considered as nonpolitical. He recognizes that elites within the latter category are capable of wielding considerable power — especially the technical elite, which is central to the military establishment — but apparently because they do not play a formal role in the determination of governmental policy, they do not qualify as political elites. *Man and His Government* (New York, 1963), pp. 316–17.

elite category of individuals outside government whose "severely sanctioned choices" directly affect the values of a large number of people. "Those who are called officials," Lasswell observes, "do not always make severely sanctioned choices, and the severely sanctioned choices are not necessarily made by persons called officials." He significantly adds that political elites include "the monopolist who is in a position to impose severe deprivations." [14] The inferences of these statements for the purposes of defining political elite are, I think, twofold: (*a*) the decisive factor in distinguishing a political elite from nonpolitical elites and non-elites is the nature of the decision rendered — not the position held by the decision-maker; and (*b*) a political-elite decision need neither be made within governmental institutions nor confined to issues closely related to government. The definition will be rounded out later in this chapter.

Again following the lead of Mosca and Pareto, Lasswell asserts that "the division into elite and mass is universal," and even in a republic, "a few exercise a relatively great weight of power, and the many exercise comparatively little." [15] It cannot be otherwise: "The discovery that in all large-scale societies the decisions at any given time are typically in the hands of a small number of people affirms a basic fact." [16] He has little difficulty in reconciling this basic fact with democracy. For, he argues, "a society may be democratic and express itself through a small leadership. The key question turns on accountability." [17]

Friedrich's position is further discussed in the latter part of this chapter. Robert Dahl is also an example of a theorist — and he has contributed a great deal to the subject — who holds to a narrow view of "political" when applied to elites. See below, p. 124.

[14] *Comparative Elites*, p. 16. In the same vein, Lasswell writes, "The scientist is accustomed to . . . recognize the possibility that what is called 'government' in one context may not correspond to the institutions that exercise effective power." "Agenda for the Study of Political Elites," in Dwaine Marvick (ed.), *Political Decisions* (Glencoe, Ill.), p. 276.

[15] *Power and Society*, p. 219.

[16] *Comparative Elites*, p. 7.

[17] *Ibid.*, p. 7.

II

Both the fundamental weakness and strength of Lasswell's concept of political elite spring from his approach to politics which he conceives as the sharing and shaping of power. First, let us examine the weakness of his position.

The definition of political elites as "the power holders of a body politic" appears, for general purposes, sound. But when we learn that a power holder is one who participates in decisions which involve "severe sanctions," its acceptability to common sense sharply diminishes. What Lasswell is saying is that the exercise of power by an elite "is simply the exercise of a high degree of coerciveness." [18] To conceive of elites as those who participate in important decisions is one thing, but to insist that these decisions — all of them — entail "severe sanctions" is to embrace the Hobbesian fallacy that political obedience is based solely on power. In permitting power to usurp the field and thus overlooking the functional concept of authority, Lasswell ignores the obvious: that most decisions are obeyed because they are regarded as authoritative, as being reasonable or potentially reasonable within the context of the value frame of those who obey.[19] Lasswell admits that if a decision is not obeyed, power has not been exercised.[20] But what he fails to understand is that compliance to a decision — even one stipulating severe sanctions for noncompliance — may also involve no exercise of power. For hardly can it be argued that a power relationship exists when B complies to A's decision not because he fears severe deprivations, but because he believes A's decision to be reasonable in terms of his own values. He complies, in other words, on the basis of authority, not power.[21]

[18] *Power and Society*, p. 98.

[19] For a discussion of the distinction between power and authority, see C. J. Friedrich, "Authority, Reason and Discretion," in C. J. Friedrich (ed.), *Authority* (Cambridge, 1958), p. 37; and Peter Bachrach and Morton S. Baratz, "Decisions and Nondecisions," *American Political Science Review* (Sept., 1963), pp. 638–39.

[20] *Power and Society*, pp. 74–75.

[21] See Robert Dahl, "The Concept of Power," *Behavioral Science* (1957), p. 205; and Bachrach and Bartaz, *op. cit.*, pp. 632–35. Lasswell of course recognizes "the inadequacy of violence alone as a stable base for the

In conceiving of authority as "formal power," Lasswell can distinguish between a king who rules and one who reigns but does not rule. But he cannot and does not distinguish between a king who rules on the basis of power and one whose rule is based on authority.[22] He is unable to make an adequate distinction here since he erroneously subsumes authority under the concept of power rather than distinguishing it as an independent and equally important concept.

Not to recognize authority as a basis for decision-making is to discount unduly the role of the people in the decision process in a democracy. A society which prides itself on its tradition of defiance against laws which are regarded as fundamentally unreasonable and arbitrary forewarns elites that their decisions must be basically reasonable (authoritative) in the eyes of the community if compliance is to be expected. Awareness by elites, in short, that constituent power can become operative if provoked minimizes the utility of decisions that rely upon severe sanctions to achieve widespread compliance. The relationship in a healthy democracy between elite and mass is more reciprocal than Lasswell's analysis would indicate. This point is obscured when power is conceived solely in terms of decisions and when the effectiveness of decisions is always attributed to severe sanctions.

Lasswell's dictum that "the division into elite and mass is universal," with the former exercising great power and the latter comparatively little, tends also to be contradicted by his explanation of the rise of autocracy. "As the power potential of the mass increases," he states, "allocation moves initially in the direction of autocracy. Under such conditions concurrence is especially important to the elite. Failure to concur may result in loss of power to the mass (rather, to a counterelite supported by the mass). Hence, whatever increases the power potential of the

---

possession and exercise of power" (*Power and Society*, pp. 121–22). But in recognizing this to be true, he does not see that a decision in conformity with the values of those who are to be affected by it is not necessarily one which involves an exercise of power. He recognizes, in other words, that "authority" is a source of power, but he does not recognize the former as a *substitute* for the latter. See *Power and Society*, pp. 121–23.

22 See *Comparative Elites*, p. 8; and *Power and Society*, p. 133.

mass will tend also to shift allocation in the direction of autocracy." [23]

In effect, he is saying that the threat of autocracy reverses the
power relationship between elite and mass, for the former, to
save its position, must concur in the demands of the latter. This
is a clear power situation in which A (the elite) is given the tacit
option by B (mass) to concur or to suffer severe deprivation –
loss of power. The fact that the mass possesses potential, as distinct from actual, power is immaterial since the threat is
sufficiently real to obtain compliance. An effective exercise of
power is never more than a threat; it is only when the threat
fails to gain compliance that severe sanctions must actually be
imposed, and then power becomes force. [24]

Thus we find that Lasswell's definition of power is not applicable to the hypothetical case which he has raised. For if
power "is participation in the making of decisions," then clearly
the mass cannot exercise power since its number and lack of
organization preclude decision-making. Hence, as the mass
acquires potential power it must be funneled into the hands of a
leader who can make a decision on its behalf and thereby exercise
power. However, on the basis of Lasswell's hypothetical case,
this line of reasoning does not necessarily follow. For the established elite may *anticipate*, as it realizes that the power potential of the mass is increasing, that if it does not act favorably to
mass demands, severe sanctions will be invoked against it. Thus
to prevent this from happening, it defers to the tacit demands of
the mass. Power, in short, can be exercised by the mass in the
absence of actual decision-making. And in this case we find
that the elite exercises relatively little power and the mass comparatively much – the complete opposite of the supposedly universal power relationship between elite and mass. This provokes
the suspicion that in a democracy, the power gap between the elite
and the mass is often not as great as Lasswell's concept of elite
would lead one to believe.

Lasswell's assumption that an increase in the power potential
of the mass enhances the probability of autocracy deserves one

[23] *Power and Society*, pp. 218, 221.
[24] See Bachrach and Baratz, *op. cit.*, pp. 635-37.

comment. This assumption is obviously valid under some circumstances, as the rise of modern totalitarianism has shown; but to imply that this is universally true is absurd. For example, widespread participation and the exercise of power by the mass during the American Revolution, the Chartist movement in England, the early stages of the New Deal in America, and the Popular Front in France strengthened and broadened constitutional democracy rather than producing autocracy. As did Kornhauser, Lasswell overlooks the distinction between the exercise of power by a demagogue supported by an aroused, alienated mass, and that by the leaders of a politically activated public who, owing to the nature and principles of the movement which they lead, are not disposed to employ undemocratic means to achieve their ends.

III

The great merit of Lasswell's power orientation to politics is that it facilitates a realistic and functional interpretation of the meaning of "political," and, more specifically, what constitutes a *political* elite. Today most political scientists recognize and in fact underscore the political nature of so-called "private governments." As Sheldon Wolin has pointed out, "No longer do legislatures, prime ministers, courts, and political parties occupy the spotlight of attention in the way they did fifty years ago. Now it is the 'politics' of the corporation, trade unions, and even universities that is being scrutinized." [25] But although political scientists are prepared to scrutinize these institutions, they are unprepared to recognize the political nature of these institutions for purposes of defining or delineating the boundaries of the political system as a whole. Thus, within this context a political system is usually thought of as comprising the rules and methods of making public policy in the form of laws, proclamations, and orders which are related to and enforced by *government*. [26] They

[25] *Politics and Vision* (Boston, 1960), p. 353.

[26] My description of the political system is paraphrased from H. B. Mayo, "How Can We Justify Democracy?" *American Political Science Review* (vol. 56, 1962), p. 555. Mayo's narrow conception of the political system, which meets the requirements of his narrow conception of democracy, is an example of what I had in mind.

tend, in other words, to accept two conflicting concepts of political: one, functionally oriented, emphasizes power relations, and the other, more static and traditional, focuses on state, government, and law. The corporation, for example, is considered a political institution when the focus of inquiry is either upon its bureaucratic apparatus — its internal conflicts and resolutions — or upon the impact of its decisions on other institutions and government. But when the subject under discussion is the meaning of democracy or political elite, the traditional and narrow concept of political is utilized. For example, Robert Dahl, in his general treatise on political science, broadly defines the political system as "any persistent pattern of human relationships that involves, to a significant extent, power, rule, or authority."[27] Under this definition it would appear reasonable to assume that political elites would include heads of corporate giants who make decisions regularly on a myriad of issues — the magnitude and rate of automation, employment policy, plant locations, allocation of philanthropic contributions, and the like — that significantly affect either the factory community directly involved, or the nation as a whole, or both. However, on the basis of his theoretical and empirical studies on elites, we find that this is not the case. In a recent paper he refers to political elites as "political leaders" and distinguishes them from economic and social elites.[28] He of course does not rule out the possibility that corporate heads or "Economic Notables," to use his term, could also be members of a political elite. But for them to qualify, it must be shown that they exercise a preponderant influence on concrete "key political decisions," and here "political" is contextually confined (though not defined) to include either decisions relating to the control of political parties or governmental decisions on such issues as urban redevelopment, public education, taxation, expenditures, and the like.[29]

[27] *Modern Political Analysis* (Englewood Cliffs, N.J., 1963), p. 6.

[28] "Power, Pluralism and Democracy: A Modest Proposal," paper delivered at the 1964 annual meeting of the American Political Science Association, Chicago, p. 3.

[29] See "A Critique of the Ruling-Elite Model," *American Political Science Review* (June, 1958), p. 469; and *Who Governs?* (New Haven, 1961), p. 64.

Of course there is no inherent reason why two or more different meanings of the same concept cannot profitably be used to fit different contextual situations. But to employ a dual meaning of political for purposes of distinguishing between decisions which relate to governmental policy and decisions which have a direct and significant influence on the public does not seem justifiable. For it can be convincingly argued, along Lasswell's line of reasoning, that differences in forms between "public" and "private" elites are overshadowed by the fact that both are engaged in decision-making that influences and shapes societal values.

Not to consider both groups as political elites is to avoid the crucial question of accountability. If, as Lasswell and others have emphasized, "in all large-scale societies the decisions at any given time are typically in the hands of a small number of people," [30] should not *all* of the small number — those in the economic and cultural as well as the political arena — be held politically accountable? Can the principle of political accountability be considered democratically sound which fails to include a comparatively significant portion of this group?

In keeping with the democratic principle that those who make decisions should be accountable to the people who are affected by them, it was reasonable for theorists of the eighteenth and nineteenth centuries to think of political as that which involved only government. There was little justification to think otherwise since government was the only organized institution that possessed sufficient decision-making power to affect large groups of people or the entire society. To continue to think in the same way today in the face of immense and powerful nongovernmental institutions that rival the power and scope of governmental decision-making is difficult to understand.[31]

[30] Lasswell, *Comparative Elites*, p. 7.

[31] "The corporate organizations of business and labor," writes Wolfgang Friedmann, "have long ceased to be private phenomena. That they have a direct and decisive impact on the social, economic, and political life of the nation is no longer a matter of argument." "Corporate Power, Government by Private Groups, and the Law," *Columbia Law Review* (vol. 57, 1957), p. 155.

One of the most interesting aspects of the dramatic confrontation of

As we have seen, Lasswell defines political elite functionally, but what he does not do is to address himself to the important question which he implicitly raises: if political elites comprise the "power holders" — both in and outside government — does not this mean that in existing democracies, especially in America, there are a significant number of institutional leaders who make "severely sanctioned choices" affecting the entire society but who are not, either directly or indirectly, held accountable to the electorate? Lasswell appears oblivious to the gap between his expanded concept of political elite and his use of the notion of accountability. When he speaks of accountability he relates it to the traditional meaning of political — that which pertains to government — and when he discusses the functional concept of political elites he is silent on the problem of accountability. For example, in *Comparative Elites* he states that "government is always government by the few, whether in the name of the few, the one, or the many. But this fact does not settle the question of the degree of democracy . . . since a society may be democratic and express itself through a small leadership. The key question turns on accountability." [32] Here, clearly, accountability is limited to government leaders. When he discusses the political elite in power terms, however, he observes that institutions other than government make "severely sanctioned choices." The problem of whether the nongovernmental institutions should be held democratically accountable is not explicitly raised. [33]

The net effect of Lasswell's analysis is to underscore a fundamental weakness in contemporary democratic theory. In emphasizing the functional concept of political elite, he highlights the inadequacy of our concept of accountability. For if political

---

President Kennedy and Big Steel in 1962 was that the President won. The fact, however, that he had to eat crow when a few months later the Steel executives announced a price increase, indicated that power relations in this sector of operations returned to normal. Another interesting aspect of the confrontation was that it showed the political nature of a matter that traditionally has been considered nonpolitical. If the initial decision to raise prices was political, is it reasonable to say that the subsequent and effective decision to raise prices was nonpolitical?

[32] *Comparative Elites*, p. 7.
[33] *Ibid.*, pp. 8, 11.

elites are societal rather than governmental in scope, then clearly the concept of accountability must be broadened commensurately. The extension of this principle would of course raise formidable problems. In the first place, Lasswell's elite concept is too loosely defined, as it stands, to serve as an adequate base for broadening accountability. To define political elites as the "power holders of a body politic" does not provide a convenient standard for delineating their boundaries. To conceive of elites statistically — in terms of the magnitude of power exercised — is not, as Carl Friedrich has pointed out, operationally useful.[34] Most businessmen make "severely sanctioned choices," but surely not all businessmen can qualify as members of political elites. This defect in Lasswell's concept of political elites can be partially rectified by using his criteria of weight (the degree to which policies are affected), and the scope of influence (the values involved).[35] That is, the distinction between political elites,` on the one hand, and nonpolitical elites and non-elites, on the other, can be judged by whether the decisions of a particular leader or a group of leaders usually affect, to a considerable degree, important societal values of a large number of persons. The distinction, however, still depends upon judgment based on empirical evidence. It is difficult to see how it could be otherwise.

Friedrich attempts to solve this problem by defining the political elite by various characteristics beyond possession of the ability to exercise a comparatively great amount of power. Thus he argues that a political elite, in addition to its ability to wield power, possesses the capacity to "effectively unite (monopolize) the rule of a particular community in their hands," and the members of the elite possess "a sense of group cohesion and a corresponding *esprit de corps,* usually expressed in cooperation." [36] A "power holder," in Lasswell's terms, whose decisions substantially influenced the shaping of important societal values for a large number of persons would not qualify as a member of a political elite under Friedrich's definition unless he also shared with a few others a monopoly of the entire rules of the community or the

---

[34] *Man and His Government* (New York, 1963).
[35] *Power and Society,* p. 73.
[36] *Man and His Government,* p. 316.

nation. By insisting that a political elite — equivalent in his terms to a governing or ruling elite — exists only if it possesses the above characteristics is to avoid the problem of identifying a political elite in a democracy. Friedrich's definition is useful in distinguishing democratic from totalitarian rule, but it is irrelevant to the question of what constitutes political elites in a democracy. The question, in effect, is ruled out by definition, leaving the operational defect of Lasswell's definition unsolved for democracies.[37]

A second defect of Lasswell's elite concept, as we have seen, is his overemphasis upon power, to the exclusion of a role for authority in the decision-making process. Thus, in allowing power to usurp the field, he, ironically, underestimates the breadth of elite decision-making. But here again, the major thrust of Lasswell's position — his insistence upon a functional approach to elites — is not impaired. All that is required is the broadening of the concept of political elite to include authority as well as power. David Easton's definition of political is sufficiently broad to include both. "Political life," Easton writes, "concerns all those varieties of activity that influence significantly the kind of authoritative policy adopted for a society and the way it is put into practice." [38] Expanding Lasswell's concept in light of Easton's definition of politics, political elites may be defined as comprising those individuals or institutions who regularly have the capacity to wield a great amount of power and authority in the form of decisions and nondecisions which significantly influence the values of a society. Since political elites invariably exercise au-

[37] Friedrich forcefully refuted the elitist positions of Mosca and Pareto more than twenty years ago in his *The New Belief in the Common Man* (Brattleboro, Vermont, 1942). But he holds substantially to the same concept as he did then, and it has little if any applicability to the current problem of clarifying the meaning of the concept for analyzing the role and power of political elites in a democracy.

[38] *The Political System: An Inquiry into the State of Political Science* (New York, 1953), p. 128. Roland Pennock and David Smith also define politics broadly: "Politics . . . refers to all that has to do with the forces, institutions, and organizational forms in any society that are recognized as having the most inclusive and final authority existing in that society for the establishment and maintenance of order, the effectuation of other conjoint purposes of its members, and the reconciliation of their differences" *Political Science* (New York, 1964).

thority, as well as power,[39] the definition has been broadened to include both concepts. However, it must be emphasized that without the power qualification of the definition, it would be somewhat difficult to distinguish between those who exercise political authority from persons who enjoy considerable authority, such as philosophers and artists, in primarily nonpolitical fields. The phrase "significantly influence" can be measured by employing Lasswell's threefold criteria of weight, scope of influence, and domain.[40] The concept of nondecisions has been included in the definition to cover those important instances where the dominant values, procedural rules, power and authoritative relations, singly or in combination, effectively prevent a latent issue from developing into a question which requires a decision. To the extent, therefore, that an individual, group, or institution participates in re-enforcing or creating a "mobilization of bias," to use Schattschneider's phrase, to prevent potentially unfavorable issues from becoming overt, the nondecision-making process is utilized.[41] It is conjectural whether Easton regarded government as the sole institution engaged in the "authoritative allocation of values," but what is significant is that he used this phrase, instead of "government" to define politics, thus raising the empirical question of whether leaders of other institutions engage both indirectly and directly in this process.

If "authoritative" is conceived as emanating solely from "formal power," following Lasswell's definition, then clearly it would be ridiculous to argue that nongovernmental institutions also authoritatively allocate values in modern society. Within the meaning of this narrow and formal concept of authority, government constitutes the exclusive agent for performing this task. However, if authority is viewed functionally, then it is logically conceivable that nongovernmental institutions also participate in performing this important task. Functionally defined, an authoritative relationship exists when both the position of the decision-maker and his

[39] For a distinction between power and authority, see pp. 118–19 above and notes cited.

[40] *Power and Society*, p. 73.

[41] For a discussion of the nondecision-making process, see Bachrach and Baratz, "Decisions and Nondecisions," *op. cit.*, pp. 641–42.

decisions are respectively regarded as legitimate and reasonable in terms of the values of those affected by the decisions. Thus the command of a policeman is authoritative to the extent that his position is regarded as legitimate *and* to the extent that his command is believed reasonably related to carrying out the responsibilities of his position. Similarly, the decisions of the board of directors of a corporation are regarded by the public as authoritative to the extent that the decisions are considered reasonable in light of the public's conception of the legitimate role of the corporation. The crucial point, in other words, is not whether the decision-maker occupies a public or private post; it is whether, in the context of public expectations, his decisions are regarded as reasonable. If they are so regarded and if, in addition, the decisions significantly affect the values of society as a whole, the decision-making institution, irrespective of its public or private image, is a political elite.

To argue that the concept of political elite is broader than government is not to deny that there are no differences between governmental and nongovernmental political elites. Government's exclusive and legitimate option to exercise physical coercion is an obvious and important distinction between the two. However, for purposes of allocating values within a society, this distinction is not significant. In the first place, most governments, especially democratic ones, are reluctant to use force on a wide scale, owing to its high political cost and its unreliability as an effective sanction. Secondly, to achieve widespread compliance with its policy, government, like other political elites, must rely primarily upon its capacity to exercise authority. It is only when its command is not authoritative — when it is unable to translate might into right — that government must resort to force. And when it does so, it is not unlikely that the next result is the re-enforcement of values hostile to governmental policy. From the standpoint, therefore, of examining the allocation of values within a political system, it is imperative that the definition of political elite be sufficiently broad to include both governmental and nongovernmental institutions.

Empirically there seems little question that heads of giant corporations are political elites. As Morton Baratz has observed, since the health of the economy is heavily dependent upon the magnitude of their expenditures on capital goods, "public policy necessarily tends to be oriented, especially over the long run, in the direction which is fundamentally in line with the interests of the giant corporate enterprises. And this will be true even if the interests of the giants are in conflict with other social goals." [42] There is also reason to believe that leaders of these mammoth organizations significantly influence societal values directly and in the short run. And once a national issue has come to public attention, they frequently exercise their influence whether they want to or not. Their sheer existence, owing to their size, power, ubiquity, and public acceptance,[43] leaves them no alternative. The response of the United States Steel Corporation to the crucial civil rights struggle in Birmingham in 1963 is a case in point. Under pressure, it declared its neutrality and thus was forced to admit to itself and to the nation that it is a separate political institution. In effect, its directors said to the public: "We realize that owing to the magnitude of our business operations in Birmingham, we are in a position to exercise a considerable amount of power and authority that, if actually exercised, would have profound effects not only on race relations in Birmingham but upon the attitudes and values of businessmen and citizens generally throughout the nation. But we believe that it is not proper for a corporation to intervene in politics." [44] But in deciding not to act in support of the integration cause, their decision favored the status quo. It was an authoritative decision in the sense that the public generally regarded it as a decision which was rightly

[42] "Corporate Giants and the Power Structure," *Western Political Quarterly* (vol. 9, 1956), p. 413.

[43] Berle believes that "the corporation, almost against its will, has been compelled to assume in appreciable part the role of conscience-carrier of twentieth-century American society." To make matters worse "the community has not created any acknowledged reference of responsibility" as a guide for its actions. *The 20-Century Capitalist Revolution* (New York, 1954), pp. 181, 182. Because of the inability of the public to provide guidance in this matter, Berle turned to the intellectual elite to provide the "transcendental margin."

[44] For Mr. Blough's statement, see *U.S. News and World Reports*, Nov. 11, 1963, p. 24.

theirs to make. Moreover, it was acceptable as well as influential, especially among members of the business community. The directors of this corporation found themselves in a position in which their decision, either way, would have widespread and profound influence upon the nation.

An interesting parallel can be drawn between the dilemma faced by the United States Steel Corporation in Birmingham and the problem confronted by President Kennedy about that time as to whether he should, to the extent that it was legally permissible, cut off the flow of federal funds to the state of Mississippi. Both the President and the corporate leaders were capable of exercising power and authority of sufficient degree to alter radically the respective situations; both decided not to act; and both, by not acting, significantly influenced the "authoritative allocation of values for a society." The parallel breaks down of course on the key question of accountability: the President was accountable to the voters and the leaders of the corporation to themselves, or as Berle would have it, to the directives of the "transcendental margin."

This type of instance — when the corporate leviathan exposes its political and self-accountable nature — is bound to occur more frequently and in sharper focus as the corporation becomes more giantlike and the economy more interdependent. It is therefore not inconceivable that the myth of being private and nonpolitical which sustains the corporation in its present form will not remain unscathed. Should not democratic theorists, especially the hardheaded realists who like to ground their theory upon facts, be prepared for such a contingency? To persist in embracing an outmoded concept and the inferences which flow from it is to allow the impersonal forces operative in our society to mold our fate.

Urbane yet tough-minded Professor Berle is quite aware that "the corporation is now, essentially, a nonstatist political institution." [45] He also knows that "American political thought has been frightened, and corporations themselves have been frightened, at any suggestion that they might emerge as political institutions in

[45] *The 20-Century Capitalist Revolution*, p. 60. In a similar vein he admitted that the corporation has "invaded the political sphere and has become in fact, if not in theory, a quasi-governing agency." *Ibid.*, p. 105.

their own and separate right." [46] It is perhaps time that political theorists take courage and recognize that the giants among these institutions are in fact political elites — political elites accountable only to themselves.

[46] *Ibid.,* p. 176.

6

Equality

"GOVERNMENTS ARE INSTITUTED among men, deriving their just powers from the consent of the governed." This statement in the Declaration of Independence is founded upon the conviction that "all men are created equal," and that each individual has a right to live his life according to his own lights and thus has a right to an equal voice in decisions which affect the whole community.[1] From these corollary principles of consent and political equality, it is not a distant jump to conceive of democracy as a system which embodies the ideal of equality of political power among all members of the community. In regarding democracy in terms of this ideal, Roland Pennock believes: "The objective of this equality (of power) is not merely the recognition of a certain dignity of the human being as such, but it is also to provide him with the opportunity — equal to that guaranteed to others — for protecting and advancing his interests and developing his powers and personality." [2]

[1] Alan Gerwin, "Political Justice," in Richard B. Brandt (ed.), *Social Justice* (Englewood Cliffs, N.J., 1962), p. 128.
[2] "Democracy and Leadership," in William Chambers and Robert Salisbury (eds.), *Democracy Today* (New York, 1962), pp. 126–27. Originally published as *Democracy in the Mid-Twentieth Century* (Saint Louis, 1960).

This ideal has given the theorists who tend toward the demo-cratic-elitist position considerable difficulty. On the one hand it is naturally attractive to any democrat, yet on the other, it funda-mentally collides with the elite-mass concept of modern industrial society. For example, Harold Lasswell's thought reflects this kind of ambivalence. As we have seen, he is quick throughout his ex-tensive writings to declare his dedication to the cause of human dignity. But he has been slow to indicate what he means by this key phrase.[3] In a significant passage in an earlier work, he does reveal in rough outline what he considers to be the relationship among dignity, democracy, and power. "Three values may be named whose proper relationship determines whether we are justi-fied in calling any group democratic. The values are power, re-spect and knowledge. Where the dignity of man is taken into account . . . such values are widely shared in a free society."[4] On the crucial question of how widely these values must be shared to determine whether the society is elitist or democratic, he is silent. Nevertheless, to suggest that the approximation of equality of power is the criterion of a free society is to challenge his basic assertion that "the division into elite and mass is uni-versal."[5] He cannot have it both ways: if political elites are permanent fixtures of society, the democratic requirement of wide sharing of the values of power, respect, and knowledge is destined to remain unrealized.

In *Power and Society*, Lasswell's view on equality becomes more circumspect; here he is careful to emphasize that "a rule is defined to be equalitarian, not in the degree to which *power* is equally distributed, but rather *access* to power."[6] To define po-litical equality as "equal eligibility to power status" nicely brings the concept of equality back in line with the major premise un-derlying democratic elitism. But the uneasy question as to whether it affords dignity to more than a few who manage to reach elite status is left unanswered. What about the great multitude who

[3] Bernard Crick, *The American Science of Politics* (London, 1959), pp. 192–97.

[4] *Analysis of Political Behavior*, p. 36, quoted in Crick, *op. cit.*, p. 195.

[5] *Power and Society*, p. 219.

[6] *Ibid.*, pp. 226, 227. Lasswell's italics.

are unsuccessful in reaching positions of power? Is their dignity saved by recognition that they had, along with everyone else, an equal opportunity to reach the top? Indeed, would not such recognition, coupled with failure, degrade rather than enhance human dignity? These are questions which democratic-elitist theory does not touch.[7]

I

To look at the issue more realistically, if equality of political power is a utopian objective, should not the principle of equality of opportunity be upgraded to take its place as an ideal or criterion of democracy? Robert Dahl, in a thoughtful and provocative paper, addresses himself to this general question.[8] As a liberal democrat, he is sympathetic to the idea of equality of political power, but as a scientist he believes that it is impossible to realize in any large political system. Consequently, he argues, to continue to espouse it as a major democratic aim is simply to further cynicism toward democracy.[9]

Dahl defines the notion of equality as follows: "Equality of power among adult citizens with respect to key governmental decisions." [10] On the basis of this formulation he proceeds to examine the principal barriers to fulfilling this criterion in large societies. In his view the familiar barriers to equality, such as the right to vote, income, wealth, status, and education, are not insurmountable. He points out that pluralistic democracies are making progress toward greater equality in these fields, and cites, with some pleasure, figures showing that distribution of income after taxes in the United States is more equally divided than in some other democratic countries, such as Sweden, Denmark, and

[7] For an interesting discussion of this point, see Roy Jenkins, "Equality," in R. H. Crossman (ed.), *The Fabian Essays* (New York, 1952), pp. 69–91.

[8] "Power, Pluralism and Democracy: A Modest Proposal," a paper delivered at the 1964 annual meeting of the American Political Science Association, Chicago, September 9–12, 1964. For an interesting contrast, see his "Equality and Power," in William V. D'Antonio and Howard J. Ehrlich (eds.), *Power and Democracy in America* (South Bend, Ind., 1961), pp. 80–89.

[9] "Power, Pluralism and Democracy," *op. cit.*, p. 14.

[10] *Ibid.*, p. 10.

Holland, where socialist and labor parties have had considerable influence.[11] More formidable barriers, he believes, are raised by differences in motivation to achieve power and differences in knowledge, information, and understanding. However, beyond these barriers is the technical difficulty connected with political decision-making in any large system. As Dahl succinctly put it: "It goes without saying that except in exceedingly small groups, specific decisions must be made by a relatively few people acting in the name of the polity." [12] Thus the criterion of equality of power "is bound to arouse expectations that large systems cannot possibly fulfill." It is ridiculous, he continues, to think nostalgically of the Rousseauian state where, owing to its smallness, the criterion is meaningful: "to argue that equality of power is possible only in very small systems still leaves unanswered the question of criteria for large systems." [13] He therefore concludes that while equality of power should not be given up as a moral goal — he recognizes that it has had great moral significance in the history of Western thought — more realistic criteria are required at this time.[14]

Before moving on to Dahl's thesis that equality of opportunity, as he has interpreted it, must be installed as a more realistic criterion, criticism of the above argument is in order. In the first place, it does not necessarily follow that because a political criterion cannot be fulfilled, it should therefore be discarded for all practical purposes. I see no reason why a principle, serving both as an ideal to strive for and as a standard for judging the progress of a political system toward the achievement of that ideal, must be realizable in practice to perform its function. The doctrine of "brotherhood of man" is beyond reach in large or small systems, but is this adequate reason to reject it as a sound principle with which to appraise human relations? Of course an unrealizable doctrine, political or religious, can lead to cynicism, but on the other hand it may be a valuable guide and a spur to a more humane society. Dahl asserts that the utopian nature of the principle of equality of political power breeds cynicism; but Roland Pen-

[11] *Ibid.*
[12] *Ibid.,* p. 12.
[13] *Ibid.,* pp. 14–15.
[14] *Ibid.,* p. 14.

nock asserts equally strongly that although it may not be fulfilled in practice, as an integral part of the democratic ideal it
has been effective in "pushing the democratic reality in the direction of equality not only of *access* to power but also equality in
the *exercise* of power." [15] Where the truth lies between these
conflicting appraisals is a question of judgment, based upon the
evidence — for surely relatively unsupported assertions one way
or the other are not sufficient to dispose of the matter. However,
owing to the possible value of the equality principle as both guide
and spur to the further democratization of society, it should not,
I believe, be discarded as an ideal or criterion in the absence of
clear evidence that it is in fact contributing to an attitude of
cynicism toward democracy.

In the second place, Dahl's examination of the criterion of
equality of power is too narrowly drawn. Obviously in large societies "key governmental decisions" must be made by a few individuals, but why must the criterion be limited to governmental
decisions? Since he, as we have seen in the last chapter, defines a
political system (and political) broadly, it would appear logical
that the political concept of equality of power might be analyzed
within this broader frame.[16] If he had done so, perhaps his answer
as to the practicality of the criterion might have been radically
different. Especially is this likely since he believes that equality of
power is theoretically possible of realization in small systems.
Thus the application of this concept of equality to nongovernmental *political* institutions becomes germane to the problem. In
other words, although it is quite clear that equality of power is
impossible of attainment in regard to "key governmental decisions," it does not foreclose its realization within subsystems of
the body politic. Thus to argue, as Dahl does, that criteria for
small systems are irrelevant — since he is concerned with criteria
for large systems — is no longer true. For if political is conceived
more broadly than encompassing governmental decision-making,

[15] "Democracy and Leadership," *op. cit.*, p. 127.
[16] *In Modern Political Analysis* (New Jersey, 1963), he states: "Contemporary political analysis tends to accept . . . a broad definition of what
is political rather than the narrow one of Aristotle. Let us therefore boldly
define a political system as follows: A political system is any persistent pattern of human relationships that involves, to a significant extent, power,
rule, or authority" (p. 6).

it can be said that the criterion of equality of power is applicable to one aspect of the system (its political subsystems) but not to another (key governmental decisions). For example, it would be applicable, on both theoretical and practical grounds, to the giant corporation. Theoretically the large corporation meets the test, as I have argued in the last chapter, of constituting a political institution whose decisions and nondecisions have a persistent and significant impact upon societal values. Practically, there is no inherent reason either why its oligarchical structure must be preserved or why the equality concept could not serve as an effective criterion to democratize the institution to a considerable degree. Of course some form of hierarchy within the institution would still be necessary, but the decision-making areas in which the criterion would be applicable are great. The major objections to a proposal of this nature will be discussed in the next chapter. Here I wish to emphasize the crucial issue of the soundness — as in the case of political elites — of defining political broadly for general purposes and narrowly for purposes of conceptualizing equality of power. It is not the inconsistency which basically concerns me, but rather the probability that the political scientist, by this self-limiting technique, forecloses to analysis whole areas which, if opened to scrutiny, might lead to rewarding insights for both political science and democracy.

II

In putting aside the notion of equality of power as being unattainable and hence unsatisfactory, Dahl believes nonetheless that a normative standard or criterion is necessary to evaluate the performance of what he calls pluralistic democracies, which, in contrast to on-going liberal constitutional systems, would "distribute some amount of power to the many." [17] He consequently

[17] "Power, Pluralism and Democracy," *op. cit.*, p. 14. His position is in sharp contrast to his past writings, in which he relied primarily upon empirical theory to defend on-going systems of polyarchy. See *Politics, Economics and Welfare*, written with Charles E. Lindblom (New York, 1953); and *A Preface to Democratic Theory* (Chicago, 1956), pp. 63–85. For a criticism of his approach to democracy, see G. Duncan and S. Lukes, "The New Democracy," *Political Studies* (vol. 11, 1963), pp. 156–77.

is not prepared to offer the traditional version of equality of opportunity as an adequate criterion for pluralistic democracies. His reluctance in this regard was not unexpected since a few years ago he remarked: "We must not be beguiled into assuming that equality of opportunity to *gain* influence will produce equality of *influence*. In fact, we are reducing and probably in the future will reduce even more many old inequalities in opportunities. But this merely insures that individuals will start out more or less even in a race for unequal influence. Even a modern dictatorship can achieve that." [18]

The criterion which he believes should be adopted to judge the system, the system that would increase the power of the many, "would prescribe that each adult citizen should have an equal and indefinitely enduring opportunity to exercise as much power over key governmental decisions as any other citizen exercises." [19] He attempts to clarify the meaning of the criterion by suggesting that it would not only apply to recruitment — "an equal opportunity to be recruited into the group of decision-makers" — but also to equality of opportunity (a) to vote, (b) to gain attention of decision-makers, and (c) "to influence the criteria of selection used in political recruitment." [20] Strictly interpreted, Dahl's criterion would be satisfied if the choice of decision-makers were more or less the same as it would be if they were chosen by lot. Put another way, it is satisfied if the various categories of voters — class, race, religion, sex, and the like — are represented by recruits proportional to their numerical strength in the population.

The differences among the three models of equality which relate to decision-making are illustrated in Figure 1. There is an equality of political power, as is shown under Model A, when all members of the community or nation participate equally in making decisions which significantly affect the values of the polity. The requirements under Model B are obtained when there is (a) equal access (in actuality) to the acquisitions (wealth, honor) and skills necessary to gain power status, and (b) equal access to positions of power. *Opportunity*, not realization, is the point of em-

---

[18] "Equality and Power," *op. cit.,* p. 87.
[19] "Power, Pluralism and Democracy," *op. cit.,* p. 17.
[20] *Ibid.,* pp. 19-20.

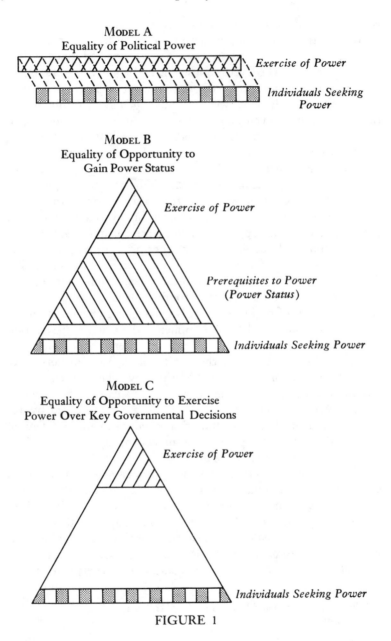

MODEL A
Equality of Political Power

Exercise of Power

Individuals Seeking
Power

MODEL B
Equality of Opportunity to
Gain Power Status

Exercise of Power

Prerequisites to Power
(*Power Status*)

Individuals Seeking Power

MODEL C
Equality of Opportunity to Exercise
Power Over Key Governmental Decisions

Exercise of Power

Individuals Seeking Power

FIGURE 1

phasis of this model. Since there are ten competitors for only one position (to follow the illustration in Figure 1), nine candidates for the post obviously will fail; but the criterion has been met if each has had an equal chance to gain the requisites to positions of power. The third model C, which corresponds to Dahl's, is similar to the second in the respect that equal *opportunity* rather than equal exercise of power is the decisive factor. It is different since each has an equal opportunity, *irrespective* of inequalities in wealth, prestige, education, etc., to exercise power. Since a democracy is concerned with values other than the distribution of power, Dahl acknowledges that some deviations from the criterion favoring, for example, intelligence, education, and probity, are bound to occur and justifiably so. Such modifications are of course warranted, but it would nevertheless move the criterion considerably closer to the traditional concept of equality of opportunity. This tendency would be true especially in a nation such as ours, where intelligence, respect, probity, and similar values are closely linked to success in pecuniary ventures. But on objective grounds alone there would be difficulty in applying the criterion. For example, there is a close correlation between education and class in most democracies; thus it would be difficult to distinguish a justifiable deviation for education against unjustifiable class bias.

If these difficulties could be solved, would the criterion, if fulfilled, actually reflect a significant increase in the power of the many? It is doubtful that it would. For the ratio between decision-makers and nondecision-makers would not — nor would have been expected to — change. To the extent, however, that elites more closely reflected the socioeconomic, racial, and other characteristics of the many, the latter's "end product" interest would probably be better served. It is likely, for example, that if the imbalance of the elite representation of lower- and lower-middle-class persons in the United States were corrected, decision-making bodies would be more responsive to the interests of this large group of the population. But again the argument rests — to reparaphrase Marcuse — on a one-dimensional view of man's interest. The elite-mass nature of society would still remain intact: the few would still count for much, exercising inordinate amounts of power, and the many, faced with a modicum of responsibility and challenge, would still count for little.

The crucial issue of democracy is not the composition of the elite — for the man on the bottom it makes little difference whether the command emanates from an elite of the rich and the wellborn or from an elite of workers and farmers. Instead the issue is whether democracy can diffuse power sufficiently throughout society to inculcate among people of all walks of life a justifiable feeling that they have the power to participate in decisions which affect themselves and the common life of the community, especially the immediate community in which they work and spend most of their waking hours and energy. Of course, "key governmental decisions" must be made by a few, but this is no reason why we should settle for a criterion for democracy which provides no guidelines to combat a rapid concentration of power outside this narrow sphere of decision-making.[21]

[21] It would appear that I criticize Kornhauser (pp. 42–46 above) for focusing his attention on the community level and Dahl for centering his analysis on "key governmental decisions" — a basic inconsistency. I do not believe that I am guilty of an inconsistency since my objection to Kornhauser's thesis is not that he considers social integration on the local level important, but rather that he believes it important for the wrong reasons — to politically insulate the masses rather than to politically extend their freedom. The latter problem is discussed in the next chapter.

7
An alternative
approach

W_{HILE IT IS TRUE} that there are many theories
of democracy,[1] it is also true that there is a general theory of
democracy which is supported by most leading theorists and
which reflects the main currents of thought in social science today. It is a theory largely explanatory rather than normative in
approach; directed toward clarifying on-going democratic systems rather than suggesting how they ought to operate. Yet it is
a theory which reflects, on the one hand, a receptiveness toward
the existing structure of power and elite decision-making in large
industrial societies, and on the other, an impatience with old myths
and sentiments associated with phrases such as "will of the people," "grass-roots democracy," and "the dignity of the common
man."

This general theory purports to be above ideology but is in
reality deeply rooted in an ideology, an ideology which is
grounded upon a profound distrust of the majority of ordinary
men and women, and a reliance upon the established elites to
maintain the values of civility and the "rules of the game" of

[1] Robert Dahl, *Preface to Democratic Theory* (Chicago, 1951), p. 1.

93

democracy. It is an ideology which is closely attached to and protective of the liberal principles embodied in the rule of law and in the rights of the individual to freedom of conscience, expression, and privacy. While embracing liberalism it rejects, in effect, the major tenet of classical democratic theory — belief and confidence in the people. The suspicion that liberalism and classical theory are fundamentally incompatible is manifested in the key explanatory concepts of democratic elitism.

Democracy conceived solely as a political method is one of these concepts. Since democracy is not seen as embodying an overriding objective, such as enhancing the self-esteem and development of the individual, the democratic-elite theorist frees himself from the charge that democratic means have failed to achieve democratic ends. He holds only that democracy must be self-perpetuating as method, and thus able to secure the open society through time. In focusing upon openness *qua* openness — avoiding the question of openness for whom — he is in a position to show that the system is in good health, while acknowledging at the same time that a large number of people are probably alienated from the social and political life around them.

While the concept of democracy as political method is not inherently elitist, it does serve as a formidable defense of the elite-mass structure of on-going democratic systems. The charge, for example, that the common man is not given sufficient opportunity to participate in meaningful decision-making and is therefore deprived of an essential means to develop his faculties and broaden his outlook is, under this concept, irrelevant. For, conceived as political method, the standard for judging democracy is not the degree of centralization or devolution in the decision-making process but rather the degree to which the system conforms to the basic principles of the democratic method: political equality (universal suffrage), freedom of discussion, majority rule, free periodic elections, and the like. When these principles are adhered to, the system is characterized by the accountability of political elites to non-elites. And in being held accountable, the former, owing to the phenomenon of anticipated reactions, normally rules in the interests of the latter. Thus, although democracy as a political method is defined in terms of procedural

principles, it invariably is defended today on the basis of its service to the interests of the people.

This defense of democracy construes the interests of the people narrowly and the democratic elite theorist has little difficulty in accepting it. He posits that the value of the democratic system for ordinary individuals should be measured by the degree to which the "outputs" of the system, in the form of security, services, and material support, benefit them. On the basis of this reasoning, the less the individual has to participate in politics on the "input" and demand side of the system in order to gain his interests on the output side, the better off he is. With rare exception elites are available to represent his interest in the decision-making process, relegating to him the comparatively painless task of paying nominal dues and occasionally attending a meeting and casting a ballot. By assuming a one-dimensional view of political interest, the democratic elitist is led to the conclusion that there is a natural division of labor within a democratic system between elite rule and non-elite interest.

By conceiving of man's political interest solely in terms of that which accrues to him from government, the democratic elitist implicitly rejects the contention of classical theorists that interests also include the opportunity for development which accrues from participation in meaningful political decisions. This two-dimensional view of political interests — interests as end results and interest in the process of participation — is rejected by the democratic elitists on the ground that it has little relevance to the reality of political life in large-scale industrial societies, and that it is based on the concept of equality of power in decision-making which is completely at odds with existing practices in modern democracies, where key political decisions must of necessity be made by a small minority. The main thrust of the elitist argument is incontestable. However, although participation in key political decisions on the national level must remain extremely limited, is there any sound reason, within the context of democratic theory, why participation in political decisions by the constituencies of "private" bureaucratic institutions of power could not be widely extended on those issues which primarily affect their lives within these institutions?

The answer to the question turns on what constitutes "political." If private organizations, at least the more powerful among them, were considered political — on the ground that they are organs which regularly share in authoritatively allocating values for society — then there would be a compelling case, in terms of the democratic principle of equality of power, to expand participation in decision-making within these organizations.[2] This

[2] The problem of what interests should be included within the corporate constituency is a difficult one, but certainly it would include the stockholders (if the corporation were privately owned), various categories of employees, suppliers, customers (would usually include the federal government), and the general consumers. To enable the latter group to be effective, it should have at its disposal extensive research facilities — including field investigators — from the Department of Consumers (the late Senator Kefauver suggested its establishment) as well as the assistance and support of the department in formulating and presenting its general policy.

Trade unions should remain, in my view, outside the corporate constituency. For if they are to represent the interests of the workers effectively, they must remain uncompromised by identification with corporate policy. As workers gain greater rights in determining policy, they will probably, as a general rule, be less in need of the protection of the union. However, unions would still perform the essential task of defending the rights of individuals and groups who are believed to have been arbitrarily or unfairly treated by the elected management. Indeed, if the corporation is to be democratic it is vital that the union serve generally as an effective opposition to the corporation. Within this sector of the political community, the union must perform the crucial task of the opposition party, but unlike the usual political party, it must remain in perpetual opposition. [See H. A. Clegg, *Industrial Democracy and Nationalization* (London, 1951), p. 145; and Adolf Sturmthal, *Workers Councils* (Cambridge, Mass., 1964), pp. 190–91.] To act in a managerial capacity they would thus undermine their vital role as opposition.

It might be argued that there is little difference between the interest of the union and the interest of workers who would be actively engaged as members of management. Thus workers' interests would be represented twice, both within and outside the corporate constituency. The argument wrongly assumes that workers, unlike other people, do not have conflict of interests as citizens, consumers, wage earners, and producers of services and goods. If doctors, lawyers, and professors have a need for outside representation (American Medical Association, American Bar Association, and American Association of University Professors), despite their engagement in managerial affairs, then it would not appear paradoxical that workers have a different interest as members of corporate boards, departmental and division committees, etc. (as producers), from their membership in the union (as wage earners).

could be achieved by radically altering their hierarchical structures to facilitate the devolution of the decision-making process. However, if one holds, as the democratic elite theorist does, to a narrow and institutional concept of political (when referring to political elites and political equality), this line of reasoning is effectively excluded from democratic theory. If "political" is confined to governmental decision-making and that which relates to it, the clearly nongovernmental institutions, irrespective of the power which they may wield and the impact of their decisions on society, are not political. And in being not political, they are exempt, as far as the reach of democratic theory goes, from democratization.

The importance to the theory of democratic elitism of interpreting narrowly the integral and key concept "political" cannot be overemphasized. First, on the basis of this interpretation, the argument for expanding democracy to encompass a portion of the economic sector can be discarded out of hand as irrelevant. Democracy is a *political* method, neither intended nor designed to operate beyond the political realm. Second, this narrow concept supports the legitimacy of the elite decision-making process within the corporations and other large private institutions. It is common knowledge that corporate elites, who regularly make decisions directly affecting social values, are accountable largely, if not solely, to themselves. But this is not considered to be an irresponsible exercise of political power since corporate managers act as private citizens on nonpolitical matters. Finally, and most important, by accepting a rigid and narrow concept of political, the elite theorist removes from consideration (within the context of democratic theory) the question of the feasibility of increasing participation in decision-making by enlarging the political scope to include the more powerful private institutions. The existing elite–non-elite relationship is consequently made immune to attack by democratic theorists loyal to the classical tradition.

If the area of politics is conceived narrowly for purposes of democratic theory, then it is understandable that the principle of equality of power, long identified as an ideal of democracy, must give way to the more realistic principle of equality of opportunity to obtain a position of power. For the former principle is only meaningful as an ideal to strive for in a society in which there is hope of obtaining a more equalitarian base for decision-making. The latter principle is suited to a political system in which power is highly stratified.

In sum, the explanatory side of democratic elite theory, in the form of its conceptualization of "method," "interest," "political," and "equality," unmistakably leads to a twofold conclusion: (a) on-going democratic systems, characterized by elite rule and mass passivity, handsomely meet the requirements of democratic theory; and (b) any suggestion that a departure from the system in the direction of obtaining a more equalitarian relationship between elites and non-elites is, on objective grounds, unrealistic.

These conclusions are in harmony with and support the normative judgment, as reflected in the writing of democratic elitists, that the illiberal propensity of the masses is the overriding threat to the free society, which, if it does survive, will do so because of the wisdom and courage of established elites. The theory of democratic elitism is not a theory of the status quo. For on the one hand it is completely in tune with the rapid change toward greater concentration of power in the hands of managerial elites, and on the other, it manifests an uneasiness that, in the absence of the creation of an elite consensus, the system is doomed.

II

Classical theory, as I emphasized at the outset of this essay, is based on the supposition that man's dignity, and indeed his growth and development as a functioning and responsive individual in a free society, is dependent upon an opportunity to participate actively in decisions that significantly affect him. The psychological soundness of this supposition has in recent years been supported by the well-known experiments contrasting the impact of authoritarian and democratic leadership on group behavior, conducted by Kurt Lewin and associates in the late 1930's,[3] by the subsequent testing of the "participation hypothesis" by numerous small group researchers,[4] and in the more speculative writ-

---

[3] For these experiments, see Kurt Lewin, Ronald Lippitt, and R. White, "Patterns of Aggressive Behavior in Experimentally Created Social Climates," *Journal of Social Psychology* (vol. 10, 1939), pp. 271–99.

[4] For a review of these studies, see Sidney Verba, *Small Groups and Political Behavior* (Princeton, 1961), pp. 216–25.

ings of Eric Fromm and others.[5] But surely one does not have to rely upon hard data to share in the belief of Rousseau, Kant, Mill, Lindsay, and others, that man's development as a human being is closely dependent upon his opportunity to contribute to the solution of problems relating to his own actions.

Although firmly grounded on what I consider to be a sound ethical position, classical theory falls short of being a viable political theory for modern society. For in underscoring the importance of widespread participation in political decision-making, it offers no realistic guidelines as to how its prescription is to be filled in large urban societies.

On its face it would appear that the democrat is left with a Hobson's choice: a theory which is normatively sound but unrealistic, or a theory which is realistic but heavily skewed toward elitism. It is my contention that he should reject both and instead accept the challenge to create a democratic theory for the twentieth century; one that is founded on the self-developmental objective and one that at the same time firmly confronts the elite-mass structure characteristic of modern societies. This approach to democracy can perhaps best be understood by contrasting it with the position of the democratic elitists in reference to certain key concepts and empirical statements that closely relate to the role of elites in a democracy. Table 7-1 on page 100 is, in summary form, an attempt to make this contrast.

At the outset the democratic theorist must abandon explanatory theory as an approach to his subject. By adhering to it he tends to accept as unalterable the configuration of society as shaped by impersonal forces. In accepting the growing concentration of elite power as given, he has been left with the task of pruning democratic theory in accord with changing conditions. Invariably this leads to support for an ideology that is strongly elitist in character. Instead, what we must acquire, as Richard Crossman has suggested, is a healthy dose of Promethean defiance against

[5] See especially *Escape from Freedom* (New York, 1941); and *The Sane Society* (New York, 1955); also see A. H. Maslow, "Power Relationship and Patterns of Personal Development," and sources cited in A. Kornhauser (ed.), *Problems in Power* (Detroit, 1957), pp. 92–131; Christian Bay, *Structure of Freedom* (Stanford, 1958), pp. 155–240.

Table 7–1   The Contrast between Democratic Elitism and
Self-Developmental Theory of Democracy

Concepts & Empirical Statement	*Democratic Elitism*	*Modern Self-Developmental*
Democracy	political method	political method and ethical end
Interest	interest-as-end-results	interest-as-end-results and interest-as-process
Equality	equality of opportunity	equality of power
Political	governmental decision-making and that which relates to it	decision-making which significantly affects societal values
Elite-mass structure of modern industrial societies	unalterable	alterable
Anti-liberal propensity of a great number of non-elites	reliance upon elites to safeguard the system	reliance upon broadening and enriching the democratic process

the illiberal and impersonal forces which tend to devastate us.[6]
To submit to those forces which threaten to emasculate democracy, to adjust values eagerly to facts as the latter turn against us, is not the attitude of the scientist but of the defeatist.[7]

Stripped of normative ends, political theory, including democratic theory, cannot perform the crucial function of providing direction to man's actions. To argue that we must be content to struggle modestly forward by combating social evil as it arises is to assume that a series of incremental moves to combat various evils will add up over time to a step forward. That need not be and often is not the case. In any event, the fundamental issue is not whether democracy should or should not have an overriding objective; it is rather whether its objective should be implicitly dedicated to the viability of a democratic elitist system or explicitly to the self-development of the individual.

[6] *The New Fabian Essays* (New York, 1952), pp. 14–15.

[7] For as Mannheim argued, the determinist — and the positivist can be included — "overlooks the fact that every major phase of social change constitutes a choice between alternatives." *Essays on the Sociology of Culture* (London, 1956), p. 169.

In opting for the latter objective, I believe that a theory of democracy should be based upon the following assumptions and principles: the majority of individuals stand to gain in self-esteem and growth toward a fuller affirmation of their personalities by participating more actively in meaningful community decisions; [8] people generally, therefore, have a twofold interest in politics — interest in end results and interest in the process of participation; benefits from the latter interest are closely related to the degree to which the principle of equality of power is realized; and progress toward the realization of this principle is initially dependent upon the acceptance by social scientists of a realistic concept of what constitutes the political sector of society.

The elite-mass structure of present-day society is very much a

[8] I am fully aware that participation will not necessarily in all cases lead to salutary results. Clearly under some conditions participation may feed the pathological needs of the participants and thereby impede development rather than facilitate it. Under other conditions, what appears to be free, meaningful discussion may in reality be a subtle process of manipulation in which the feelings and thoughts of those participating are induced by the leader. [Eric Fromm, *Escape from Freedom* (New York, 1941), p. 210.] This technique is an effective way of controlling without revealing the source of control. [See Sidney Verba, *Small Groups and Political Behavior* (Princeton, 1961), p. 217–25.] In an age where individuals are particularly sensitive to the demands and values of others, participation that is free of manipulation may nonetheless contribute to the prevalent tendency to "cut everyone down to size who sticks up or sticks out in any direction." [David Riesman, *The Lonely Crowd* (New Haven, 1950).]

Admittedly these dangers exist. But they do not vitiate the assumption regarding the value of participation. They do however raise two important questions: Under what concrete conditions will man's capacities be developed and under what conditions will development be frustrated? How will democratic theory provide the developmental conditions? Definitive answers to these questions must await empirical research. Tentatively, however, I would suggest that beneficial results from participation can best be assured if two conditions are present: (*a*) that the participants are roughly equal in the power they are capable of exerting in the decision-making process; (*b*) that diverse interests are represented within the participating group. The first condition would tend to prevent manipulation and the second would tend to prevent the pressures of conformity from being overbearing on those sharing in the decision-making process. Democratic theory must therefore include among its principles equality of power and pluralism.

reality. But it is an unalterable structure only if political decision-making is viewed narrowly, as governmental decision-making. I have argued that such a view is untenable, that the evidence will simply not support a *twofold* definition of political. To define political broadly for general purposes and then, when concerned with the meaning of political elites or political equality, to retreat to a nineteenth-century notion of the concept is to remove an important area of politics from political research. If the political scientist is to be realistic, he must recognize that large areas within existing so-called private centers of power are political and therefore potentially open to a wide and democratic sharing in decision-making.

It is true that political scientists of all persuasions are very willing to analyze both the power structure of "private governments" and the interaction of these units with government policy. But these institutions are distinguished from government on the ground that they, unlike the latter, do not possess the exclusive and legitimate right to exercise force. Of course this is a valid distinction, but is it sufficient to exempt private governments from scrutiny within the context of the democratic norms of political equality, popular participation in the formulation of basic policy, and accountability of leaders to lead? I do not believe so. Obviously General Motors is not the United States government. However, there is a basic similarity between the two: they both authoritatively allocate values for the society. It is on the basis of this similarity that General Motors and other giant private governments should be considered a part of the political sector in which democratic norms apply. Within the context of constitutional law, a private firm which performs a public function is subject, like the government, to the limitations of the Constitution.[9] The expansion of the concept of "state action" by the Supreme Court, which has had a significant effect in constitutionalizing private governments, reflects the Court's insistence that the Constitution will be a viable instrument to meet the needs of the present. It is time that democratic theorists emulate the spirit of their judicial brethren. They may begin by holding that when a

[9] See *Marsh v. Alabama*, 326 U.S. 501 (1946), *Terry v. Adams*, 345 U.S. 461 (1953), and Arthur Miller, *Private Governments and the Constitution* (Center for the Study of Democratic Institutions, Santa Barbara, Cal., 1959).

private government performs a public function — such as authoritatively allocating values for society or a large part of it — that for purposes of democratic theory as well as constitutional law, it is considered a political institution and thus within the reach of the Constitution *and* democratic principles.

It might be asked, why is it necessary to politicize private centers of power in order to broaden the base for participation? Does not the argument erroneously assume that ordinary men and women actually desire a greater share in shaping policies which affect them? If this were the case, one would think that the people would have already exploited to the fullest every opportunity to engage in politics within existing political institutions. As one study after another has shown, a comparatively large portion of the public is indifferent to politics; they abstain from voting, they are virtually ignorant of public affairs, and they lack a strong commitment to the democratic process. Would not this same pattern of indifference exist within a broadened political area?

If the newly recognized political sector were the factory, the office, the enterprise, I do not believe this would be the case. For many individuals political issues and elections appear either trivial or remote and beyond the reach of their influence. Of a different magnitude are issues which directly affect them in their place of work, issues which are comparatively trivial, yet are overlaid with tensions and emotions that often infuriate and try men's souls. It is here — despite the legitimatizing effects of bureaucratic forms — that the ugliness of man's domination of man is fully revealed, and it is here, consequently, that democracy must become established and put to use. I am not suggesting that the average worker, for example, if given the opportunity to share in the making of factory decisions, would be magically transformed, in the fashion of Rousseau's common man, from an unimaginative, parochial, selfish human being to a broad-minded, intelligent, public-spirited citizen. I am saying that political education is most effective on a level which challenges the individual to engage cooperatively in the solution of concrete problems affecting himself and his immediate community. In the past this task was ideally performed in the New England town meeting; in twentieth-century America it can effectively be performed in the factory community.

Clearly the highly complex, mammoth industrial corporate

structure of today has little resemblance to the town meetings of eighteenth-century America. This does not mean, however, that the modern corporation could not, to a significant extent, be democratized in line with the principles and objectives that I have outlined above. Admittedly at this point it is a matter of conjecture whether such an undertaking, from both a political and economic standpoint, is workable. However, in my view, it borders on dogmatism to reject this challenge out of hand, on the assertion, for example, that the principles of accountability and equality of power are irreconcilable, or that the devolution of decision-making is, without serious loss of efficiency, impossible within the modern industrial firm. We cannot, with any degree of confidence, extrapolate a democratic scheme for modern industry from on-going oligarchic institutions. It seems equally evident that we cannot, with any degree of confidence, conclude from observation of oligarchic practices that such a democratic scheme, if put into practice, would be doomed to failure. If democracy is to be taken seriously, we cannot remain on dead center on this issue. What is called for, at minimum, is discussion and debate on various aspects of the question with the view of possible experimentation with nationalization of one or a few corporate political giants.[10] Serious consideration of such a proposal can no longer

[10] Contrary to the view of some students, the British experience in nationalization of industry is not indicative that the democratization of large-scale industries is impossible. From the outset of the postwar experience, the Labor Party opted for centralization of control with no attempt to inaugurate a system of workers' participation beyond a warmed-over Whitney scheme of "joint consultation" on a strictly advisory basis between trade union officials and management. It is true that despite vigorous and prolonged discussion during the interwar years between Fabians and Guild Socialists, the Labor Party was unable to resolve the contradiction between the principles of political accountability and workers' participation in decision-making. But this is not surprising since neither side in the discussions ever succeeded in coming to the heart of the issue. The scheme of workers' control advocated by G. D. H. Cole and his school excluded governmental and consumer representation in the control of industry on the erroneous belief that workers represented the interests of the entire society. Thus they never came to grips with the problem of integrating political accountability and industrial democracy. The Fabians, whose view eventually prevailed, naïvely assumed that since the essence of democracy is parlia-

be left to socialists, nor should controversy centering on such a proposal be fought along traditional socialist-capitalist lines of argument. Today, argument along those lines would border on the irrelevant. For the fundamental issue no longer relates to the problem of production or distribution but to the problem of power.

The illiberal and anti-democratic propensity of the common man is an undeniable fact that must be faced. But to face it realistically is not, as I have attempted to show, to rely upon elites to sustain the system. For in the first place, there is little evidence that elites, any more than non-elites, are prepared to defend procedural rights at the risk of jeopardizing their own personal status, prestige, and power. Secondly, to assume a harmony be-

mentary representation of majority will, the legal transformation of a factory from private to public would somehow gratify the men who worked in it and further the cause of democracy. In effect, they held that the problem of worker participation in the management of industry could be dispensed with since the workers, as other groups in society, are effectively represented by their party in Parliament. The validity of this contention aside, they, in the manner of democratic elitists, were basically in error in their presupposition that man's political interests are "one-dimensional" — all that is required is that his interest-as-results be adequately represented. The widespread disillusionment with the Labor Party's program of nationalization among workers in existing nationalized industries stems largely from this error. [See R. Crossman, *Socialist Values in a Changing Civilization* (Fabian Tract 286, London, 1955).] However, even if the Party's leaders had seen the issue differently, it is extremely doubtful that, owing to the plight of the British economy after the war, there would have been an opportunity to engage in significant experimentation in the devolution of the decision-making process in industry. A persisting imbalance of payments and widespread obsolescence of industry, among other factors, compelled the Labor government to focus on the immediate task of expanding Britain's productive capacity. Thus, as G. D. H. Cole said in another context, "We cannot afford to risk failure and confusion by trying to be too 'democratic' at the very start." [Quoted by Dahl, "Workers' Control of Industry and the British Labor Party," *American Political Science Review* (vol. 148, 1947), p. 889.] The profound disappointment among observers of the British experience with democratization of industry is that the Labor Party, despite pressure from some unions and intellectuals, has not since, nor is it now prepared, to take the risk. But the claim that it is still saddled with severe economic problems, which inhibit its capacity to experiment, still has considerable validity.

tween the vested interests of elites and the well-being of democracy is to sap the latter of the boldness and imaginativeness characteristic of democracies of the past. To do so would be to confine the expansion of democracy to an area where it does not threaten the basic substantive interests of dominant elites. Thirdly, it is difficult to understand how elites, who have conflicting substantive interests, can reach a consensus sufficiently effective to safeguard democracy from attack. Finally, assuming elites can reach such a consensus, it seems doubtful that they could generate sufficient power *democratically* to restrain the excessive demands and actions of the undemocratic mass and its leaders.

If it is time to abandon the myth of the common man's allegiance to democracy, it is also time that elites in general and political scientists in particular recognize that without the common man's active support, liberty cannot be preserved over the long run. The battle for freedom will be lost by default if elites insulate themselves from the people and rely on countervailing forces, institutional and social barriers, and their own colleagues to defend the system from the demagogic leader of the mob. Democracy can best be assured of survival by enlisting the people's support in a continual effort to make democracy meaningful in the lives of all men.

Index